TREES OF GREEN LAKE

TREES OF GREEN LAKE

Arthur Lee Jacobson

© 1992 Arthur Lee Jacobson
All rights reserved
Printed in the United States of America
First printing April, 1992

Library of Congress Catalog Card Number 92-90201
ISBN: 0-9622918-1-1

Cover photos © Arthur Lee Jacobson
(Front: Ringleaf Weeping Willow; back: Coast Redwood)
Cover design by the author and Stephen Herold
Design & Typography by Stephen Herold
Typesetting by Lasergraphics

Other titles by the same author:

Trees of Seattle (1990)
Trees of the Bloedel Reserve (1992)
Purpleleaf Plums (a Timber Press publication to be released in late 1992 or 1993)

Arthur Lee Jacobson
2215 E. Howe Street
Seattle, WA 98112

CONTENTS

Illustration Credits vi
Acknowledgements vii
INTRODUCTION 9
    The intent of the essays................................ 9
    The 162 trees present today 10
    Native trees 14
    Abbreviated history of the park 14
    Measurements of the park 16
    Wild vegetation other than trees 16
    Seasonal changes; calendar............................ 18
TOURING THE PARK'S TREES 23
    East area—fieldhouse, pool, parking lot, ballfields, tennis 23
    Northeast shore—Bald Cypress territory 26
    North tip—wading pool and vicinity 27
    Northwest area—the trees at their best 28
    Western strip—by busy Aurora 30
    Southwest—below Woodland Park 30
    South—Aqua Theatre and Pitch n' Putt golf course 31
    Southeast—narrow strip with few trees 32

A to Z TREE ACCOUNTS 33

INDEX 166

Illustration Credits

From: Michael Lee, Landscape Architect.
42, 45, 58, 65, 77, 79, 80, 82, 93, 96, 115, 116, 122, 134, 135, 136, 138, 141, 154, 158, 160.

From: *Trees of the Northern United States* by Austin Craig Apgar. New York: American Book Co. 1892.
34, 46, 48, 50, 51, 54, 63, 68, 73, 84, 86, 88, 89, 90, 92, 94, 98, 99, 100, 102, 107, 112, 114, 120, 137, 149, 151, 152, 153, 155, 165.

From: *Ornamental Shrubs of the United States* by Austin C. Apgar and Ada Apgar Draycott. New York: American Book Co. 1910.
33, 40, 47, 49, 69, 72, 74, 75, 76, 81, 83, 90, 91, 95, 97, 104, 105, 108, 111, 128, 143, 144, 145, 146, 163.

From: *Handbuch der Nadelholzkunde* by Ludwig L. Beissner. Berlin: Paul Parey. 1909.
41, 55, 74.

From: *A Manual of the Flowering Plants of California* by Willis Linn Jepson. Berkeley: Associated Students Store. 1925.
43, 53, 56, 66, 78, 85, 106, 140, 150, 156.

From: *Veitch's Manual of the Coniferæ* by Adolphus H. Kent. 2nd ed. London: James Veitch & Sons. 1900.
87, 142, 164.

From: *Arboretum et Fruticetum Britannicum* by John C. Loudon. 2nd ed. 8 volumes. London: Henry G. Bohn. 1854.
54, 67, 125, 131, 148, 157.

From: *Wayside and Woodland Trees* by Edward Step. London: Frederick Warne. 1904.
44, 52, 59, 103, 123, 139, 162.

From: *Forest Trees of the Pacific Slope* by George B. Sudworth. Washington, D.C.: U.S.D.A. 1908.
101, 129, 132.

From: *Trees, The Yearbook of Agriculture 1949*. Washington, D.C.: U.S.D.A. 1949.
44, 48, 109, 110, 113, 117, 118, 119, 121, 130, 133, 147, 155, 159.

Acknowledgements

Madelon Bolling edited the book, demonstrating again an admirable aptitude to improve my blemished sentences. Readers, not seeing the pages marked red with corrections, may unfairly credit me with more writing skill than I possess. Scott Cline, the City Archivest, made available historic records. Steve Herold was indispensable in the book's design and production. Joy Jacobson, my sister, drew the map. Michael Lee offered helpful advice upon reviewing an early draft of the book, catching what would have otherwise been some embarrassing blunders. Martin Muller, the Green Lake bird expert, also gave freely of his treasury of information. Bob Van Pelt measured some trees.

Some of the material that I wrote in November, 1990, for the Friends of Seattle's Olmsted Parks' *newsletter*, is reused in the present volume. If you like Seattle's parks and want to enjoy them more fully, become familiar with this organization; contact them at P.O. Box 15984, Seattle, Washington, 98115-0984.

INTRODUCTION

Every park should have a book like this. All of its trees are embraced in these pages, and in plain, vigorous words they come alive. Readers can depend on the essays to contain the essential facts about each tree, and can view the living specimens for first-hand acquaintance.

Green Lake is Seattle's favorite park, so regardless of what kind of tree population it has, visitors care. But the park has a large, varied and fascinating tree collection, which partly accounts for the popularity of the place. In March 1992, there were 2,472 trees there, of 162 different kinds. This book serves as a voice for these trees. Just as good cooks love sharing their meals with friends, and musicians crave an audience, so "tree gurus" need to express messages of green wonder. If you find greater enjoyment and meaning in life by becoming more aware about trees, then we have succeeded together.

What *use* is such tree information? Certainly people cannot get rich by becoming more intimate with trees. Love, however, cares not—birdwatchers, mushroom-pickers, wildflower enthusiasts and general outdoors devotees find their reward in long hours of pleasure; new discoveries thrill the spirit and give a burst of energy to the body. In other words, although useless for fanfare or pecuniary wealth, trees offer plenty. They stand in quiet solitude, sunlight glowing on their trunks, nature's scents pervading the air. People respond to the waiting trees one way or another, and this book is intended for the sympathetic contingent.

The intent of the essays.

Green Lake trees are chiefly ornamental, so the many brief essays comprising this book stress their appearance. Everyone knows, of course, that trees also cleanse the air, moderate the climate, provide cooling shade, yield indispensable products, and a host of other environmental and economic benefits. However, to even mention, let alone detail, all the uses of each species would make this book damnably clumsy. Above all, the essays strive to bring out a suggestion of each tree's "personality," serving as a friendly introduction. Some trees favored by the writer are praised enthusiastically in these prose portraits, while other trees, as it were, are depicted in dirty rags. "What!" you may exclaim, "can this be fair?" Even if the wording *were* devoid of passion or art, and was limited instead to a cold, detached recording of facts, it would not change the fact that certain trees *do* have irrepressibly distinctive "flavors," and humans, whether we like it or not, react to them. To suppress my interpretation altogether in order to give you a smooth, unvaried succession of tree accounts, would be like giving you a meal with no pronounced zest, no spices, no condiments—it would nourish your body but not please your tongue. If my trees are here served in prose too syrupy, too thick, sweet and rich, then at least my writing has avoided the extreme of sterility common in government and academic circles, only to suffer the opposite extreme of cheesecake overdose. Be that as it may, my *intent* was that elusive ideal blend of classicism and romanticism: facts served with sauce.

The 162 trees present today.

In December, 1991, a tree census was conducted at Green Lake. The goal was to count and identify every tree. The results were near the intention, but a few exceptions had to be made. Duck Island was excluded. Small, wild seedlings were ignored. Although both Norway and Sycamore Maples have *purpleleaf* specimens at the park, they could not be distinguished. Finally, the numerous, tightly crowded willows could not all be accounted for. Thus, as of March 1992, the total number of different kinds of trees noted is 162. This is an easy number to adjust as needed in the future. The *total number* of trees is much more tenuous and will quickly become dated. Both Mother Nature and the Seattle Parks Department work on destroying some trees and adding others every year. In the following list, **N** signifies the tree is native in Seattle (15 total), and **W** means it grows wild at Green Lake (22 total).

82	N	W	ALDER, Red	*Alnus rubra*
2			APPLE, Orchard	*Malus domestica*
1			APPLE, European Crab-	*Malus sylvestris* 'Plena'
8			APPLE, Kaido or Midget Crab-	*Malus* × *micromalus*
22			APPLE, Purple Crab-	*Malus* × *purpurea*
2			APPLE, Red Jewell™ Crab-	*Malus* Red Jewell™
20			APPLE, Redvein Crab-	*Malus Niedzwetzkyana*
9			APPLE, Siberian Crab-	*Malus baccata*
6			ARBORVITÆ, Oriental	*Thuja orientalis*
6			ARBORVITÆ, Pyramidal	*Thuja occidentalis* 'Fastigiata'
1			ASH, Caucasian or Narrowleaf	*Fraxinus oxycarpa*
2	N		ASPEN, Quaking	*Populus tremuloides*
9			BEECH, European	*Fagus sylvatica*
23		W	BIRCH, Downy	*Betula pubescens*
1			BIRCH, Downy *hybrid*	*Betula* × *aurata*
11	N		BIRCH, Paper or Canoe	*Betula papyrifera*

78	W	BIRCH, White	*Betula pendula*
7		BIRCH, Weeping White	*Betula pendula* 'Tristis'
1		BUCKEYE, Yellow or Sweet	*Æsculus octandra*
1		CATALPA, Northern	*Catalpa speciosa*
3		CATALPA, Southern	*Catalpa bignonioides*
1		CEDAR, Atlas	*Cedrus atlantica*
19		CEDAR, Blue Atlas	*Cedrus atlantica* f. *glauca*
17		CEDAR, Deodar	*Cedrus Deodara*
28		CEDAR, Incense	*Calocedrus decurrens*
6		CEDAR of Lebanon	*Cedrus libani*
4	N	CEDAR, Western Red	*Thuja plicata*
31		CEDAR, Zebra	*Thuja plicata* 'Zebrina'
1	N W	CHERRY, Bitter	*Prunus emarginata*
23		CHERRY, Higan	*Prunus subhirtella*
2		CHERRY, Horinji	*Prunus* 'Horinji'
95		CHERRY, Kwanzan	*Prunus* 'Kwanzan'
16	W	CHERRY, Mazzard	*Prunus avium*
1		CHERRY, Mikuruma-gaeshi	*Prunus* 'Mikuruma-gaeshi'
1		CHERRY, Naden	*Prunus* × *Sieboldii*
1		CHERRY, Ojochin	*Prunus* 'Ojochin'
3		CHERRY, Oshima	*Prunus Lannesiana*
7		CHERRY, Shiro-fugen	*Prunus* 'Shiro-fugen'
6		CHERRY, Shirotae or Mt. Fuji	*Prunus* 'Shirotae'
1		CHERRY, Sour *hybrid*	*Prunus* × *Gondouinii* 'Schnee'
3		CHERRY, Temari	*Prunus* 'Temari'
14		CHERRY, Ukon	*Prunus* 'Ukon'
1		CHERRY, Whitcomb	*Prunus subhirtella* 'Whitcombii'
41		CHERRY, Yoshino	*Prunus* × *yedoensis*
67	N W	COTTONWOOD, Black	*Populus trichocarpa*
102		CYPRESS, Bald	*Taxodium distichum*
2		CYPRESS, Hinoki	*Chamæcyparis obtusa*
58		CYPRESS, Lawson	*Chamæcyparis Lawsoniana*
2		CYPRESS, Lawson Blue	*C. Lawsoniana* f. *glauca*
8		CYPRESS, Lawson Scarab	*C. Lawsoniana* 'Allumii'
2		CYPRESS, Lawson Weeping	*C. Lawsoniana* 'Intertexta'
7		CYPRESS, Leyland	× *Cupressocyparis Leylandii*
35		CYPRESS, Sawara	*Chamæcyparis pisifera*
3		CYPRESS, Sawara Gold	*C. pisifera* 'Aurea'
9		CYPRESS, Sawara Moss	*C. pisifera* f. *squarrosa*
20		CYPRESS, Sawara Plume	*C. pisifera* f. *plumosa*
9		CYPRESS, Sawara Thread	*C. pisifera* f. *filifera*
2		DOGWOOD, Cornelian-Cherry	*Cornus mas*
20		DOGWOOD, Eastern	*Cornus florida*
1		DOGWOOD, Eastern Pink	*Cornus florida* f. *rubra*
13		DOGWOOD, Kousa	*Cornus Kousa*
4	N W	DOGWOOD, Pacific	*Cornus Nuttallii*
5		ELM, American White	*Ulmus americana*
1		ELM, Hybrid	*Ulmus* × *hollandica*
5		ELM, Siberian	*Ulmus pumila*

2		ELM, Smoothleaf	*Ulmus minor*
1		FIG, Common	*Ficus Carica*
4		FIR, Caucasian	*Abies Nordmanniana*
110	N W	FIR, Douglas	*Pseudotsuga Menziesii*
2		FIR, Greek	*Abies cephalonica*
19		FIR, Veitch	*Abies Veitchii*
11		FIR, White	*Abies concolor*
5		GINKGO	*Ginkgo biloba*
26	W	GOLDENCHAIN	*Laburnum anagyroides*
7		GOLDENCHAIN, Alpine	*Laburnum alpinum*
13	W	GOLDEN RAIN TREE	*Koelreuteria paniculata*
1		HAWTHORN, Autumn Glory	*Cratægus* 'Autumn Glory'
29		HAWTHORN, Cockspur	*Cratægus crus-galli*
54	W	HAWTHORN, Common	*Cratægus monogyna*
1		HAWTHORN, Paul's Scarlet	*Cratægus lævigata* 'Paul's Scarlet'
27		HAWTHORN, Red	*Cratægus lævigata* 'Punicea'
9	W	HOLLY, English	*Ilex Aquifolium*
1		HORNBEAM, European	*Carpinu Betulus*
6		HORSE-CHESTNUT, Common	*Æsculus Hippocastanum*
1		HORSE-CHESTNUT, Red	*Æsculus* × *carnea*
3		JUNIPER, Rocky Mountain	*Juniperus scopulorum*
66		LARCH, European	*Larix decidua*
6		LARCH, Japanese	*Larix Kaempferi*
3		LOCUST, Black	*Robinia Pseudoacacia*
2		LOCUST, Globe	*R. Pseudoacacia* 'Umbraculifera'
5		MAGNOLIA, Evergreen	*Magnolia grandiflora*
2		MAGNOLIA, Star	*Magnolia stellata*
18	N W	MAPLE, Bigleaf	*Acer macrophyllum*
1		MAPLE, English	*Acer campestre*
3		MAPLE, Japanese	*Acer palmatum*
1		MAPLE, Japanese Purpleleaf	*Acer palmatum* cultivar
86	W	MAPLE, Norway	*Acer platanoides*
?		MAPLE, Norway Schwedler	*Acer platanoides* 'Schwedleri'
92	W	MAPLE, Sycamore	*Acer Pseudoplatanus*
?		MAPLE, Sycamore Wineleaf	*Acer Pseudo.* 'Atropurpureum'
2	N	MAPLE, Vine	*Acer circinatum*
28	W	MOUNTAIN ASH, Common	*Sorbus aucuparia*
3		MOUNTAIN ASH, Big-berry	*Sorbus aucuparia* form
1		OAK, Black	*Quercus velutina*
4		OAK, Bur	*Quercus macrocarpa*
1		OAK, Daimyo	*Quercus dentata*
2		OAK, Oriental White	*Quercus aliena*
5		OAK, Pin	*Quercus palustris*
11		OAK, Red	*Quercus rubra*
4		OAK, Scarlet	*Quercus coccinea*
1		OAK, Swamp White	*Quercus bicolor*
1		OAK, White	*Quercus alba*
1		OAK, White *hybrid*	*Quercus* × *Bebbiana*
1		PHOTINIA, Chinese	*Photinia serrulata*

25		PINE, Austrian Black	*Pinus nigra*
18		PINE, Chinese	*Pinus tabulæformis*
53		PINE, Eastern White	*Pinus Strobus*
1		PINE, Himalayan White *hybrid*	*Pinus Wallichiana* hybrid
4		PINE, Japanese Black	*Pinus Thunbergiana*
90		PINE, Japanese Red	*Pinus densiflora*
1		PINE, Mountain	*Pinus uncinata*
8		PINE, Mugo	*Pinus Mugo*
6		PINE, Ponderosa	*Pinus ponderosa*
1		PINE, Red	*Pinus resinosa*
91		PINE, Scots	*Pinus sylvestris*
16	N	PINE, Shore	*Pinus contorta*
8		PINE, Tanyosho	*Pinus densiflora* 'Umbraculifera'
53		PLANE or SYCAMORE, Hybrid	*Platanus* × *hybrida*
1		PLUM, Cherry	*Prunus cerasifera*
4		PLUM, Moser Purpleleaf	*Prunus* × *blireiana* 'Moseri'
3		PLUM, Pissard Purpleleaf	*Prunus cerasifera* 'Pissardii'
1		PLUM, Purple Pony™	*Prunus cerasifera* 'Purple Pony'™
5		POPLAR, Lombardy Black	*Populus nigra* 'Italica'
30		POPLAR, Weeping Simon	*Populus Simonii* 'Pendula'
1		POPLAR, White	*Populus alba* 'Nivea'
6		REDWOOD, Coast	*Sequoia sempervirens*
3		REDWOOD, Dawn	*Metasequoia glyptostroboides*
22		REDWOOD, Sierra	*Sequoiadendron giganteum*
1		SERVICEBERRY	*Amelanchier arborea*
9		SILK TREE	*Albizia Julibrissin*
1		SNOWBELL TREE, Japanese	*Styrax japonicus*
5		SORREL TREE	*Oxydendrum arboreum*
3		SPRUCE, Colorado	*Picea pungens*
15		SPRUCE, Colorado Blue	*Picea pungens* f. *glauca*
73		SPRUCE, Norway	*Picea Abies*
9		SPRUCE, Oriental	*Picea orientalis*
9	N	SPRUCE, Sitka	*Picea sitchensis*
19		SWEETGUM	*Liquidambar Styraciflua*
20		TULIP TREE	*Liriodendron Tulipifera*
56	W	WALNUT, Black	*Juglans nigra*
2		WILLOW, Corkscrew	*Salix Matsudana* 'Tortuosa'
±50	W	WILLOW, Goldtwig	*Salix alba* var. *vitellina*
23	N W	WILLOW, Pacific Black	*Salix lasiandra*
5		WILLOW, Ringleaf Weeping	*Salix babylonica* 'Crispa'
1	N W	WILLOW, Scouler Pussy	*Salix Scouleriana*
9	W	WILLOW, Sepulchral Weeping	*Salix* × *sepulcralis*
7	N W	WILLOW, Sitka Pussy	*Salix sitchensis*
1		WILLOW, White	*Salix alba*
2		WILLOW, White *hybrid*	*Salix* × *rubens*
7		WITCH-HAZEL	*Hamamelis virginiana*
5		YEW, English	*Taxus baccata*
15		ZELKOVA	*Zelkova serrata*

2,472 total

Native trees.

Fifteen species present at the park are native. This means their natural distribution or range covers Seattle, and specimens grew here before settlers arrived in the 1850s. It usually means that *wild* specimens are currently growing at Green Lake.

ALDER, Red	MAPLE, Bigleaf
ASPEN, Quaking	MAPLE, Vine
BIRCH, Paper	PINE, Shore
CEDAR, Western Red	SPRUCE, Sitka
CHERRY, Bitter	WILLOW, Pacific Black
COTTONWOOD, Black	WILLOW, Sitka
DOGWOOD, Pacific	WILLOW, Scouler
FIR, Douglas	

None is remarkable for rarity. Two curiously abundant native species absent from the park are Oregon Ash (*Fraxinus latifolia*), frequent by lakes and rivers generally; and one of the city's commoner wetland pussy willows, *Salix Piperi*. Remember that native species are not always wild—sometimes we plant them. Moreover, introduced species such as Holly or Mountain Ash run wild here. Of the wild herbaceous and shrubby vegetation around Green Lake, most of the dozens of species are non-native. If Green Lake was somehow limited solely to native plants it would be far less stimulating as well as weaker ecologically. It would be a dank, dreary woodland dominated by alders, bushy willows and mammoth cottonwoods. The coarse croak of the raven might be heard, whilst the humming sound of humanity would be muffled by the less spirited atmosphere.

Abbreviated history of the park.

In 1900 the lake was much larger than it is now: its shoreline extended southward all the way to N 54th Street. Between 1905 and 1912 the City of Seattle purchased the surrounding lands, thereby causing some property owners to turn livid with indignation. It was largely at the behest of the Olmsted Brothers Landscape Architecture firm, of Brookline, Massachusetts, that Seattle chose to act. The Olmsteds encouraged city park planners to fill the growing city with public parks, boulevards and vistas for people to enjoy. At the time, of course, this was visionary. Green Lake was an unimproved swampy area of alder trees and mosquitos. Few people lived near it.

The Olmsted proposals for developing Green Lake from a swamp into a first-rate park, included all facets: contouring and topography, road, building and facility placement—but primarily *tree planting*. As the work was carried out over many years, was based partly on verbal instruction, and surviving documents are scarce and scattered, when the question is asked today whether a given Green Lake tree owes its existence to the Olmsted Brothers, we can rarely give a definite answer.

During 1910, major street leveling and even pouring of concrete was done in the area. This set the stage for the monumental task of lowering the lake level about 7 feet and shrinking its size dramatically, which had to be done if there was to be *room* for park land. Between 1911 and 1915 dredging, dike-building and filling was done to accomplish the shrinking of the water area and increase of land area. It was a giant, muddy mess.

In 1915 the boulevard was paved; the next year a dump was started to fill in the area east of the lake that now has the ballfields.

1919 saw the planting of Black Walnut trees lining West Green Lake Way. These commemorated local soldiers killed in the first World War.

1927–28: The bathhouse was built.

1929: The fieldhouse was constructed on garbage fill with a foundation of pilings. Dedicated October 11th. A new driveway to it (near Latona Street and still in use) replaced the original one.

1930: The local Japanese Association of America donated 3,500 Japanese flowering cherry trees to the Park Department, many of which would be planted at Green Lake in the next couple of years.

1931: 100 crab-apple trees were donated by the Seattle Garden Club.

1932: To make way for Aurora Avenue, fill dirt from the excavation of Woodland Park was dumped to raise low spots of the new park. Also this year, four American elms and some of the crab-apples were planted to honor the bicentennial of George Washington's birth.

1933: Cinders were laid to make a 10 foot wide path around the lake.

1934 saw much landscaping, including the Cedars of Lebanon by the northwest tennis courts.

1936: Duck Island was built as a wildlife reserve.

1944: A fuss was raised over the cutting of willows that served as roosts for purple martins, a bird that was common at the time but far less so now because of the starling invasion.

1945: Children's fishing pier was constructed near the fieldhouse.

1947: Pitch n' Putt golf course was graded, constructed, planted.

1948: Restrooms at the north end of the park were built.

1950: The Aqua Theatre and adjacent shellhouse were built.

1954: Evans Pool was built.

1959: The concession and restrooms by the Aqua Theatre were built.
1966: The pier was built east of the Aqua Theatre.
1968: The path around the lake was paved with asphalt.
1970: The Bathhouse Theatre renovation and opening.
1970: A children's play area was made northeast of the Evans Pool.

Measurements of the park.

At present, the average water depth is 12.7 feet; the maximum depth about 29 feet. The path distance is 2.83 miles. The land area is 86.6 acres; the water area 255.3 acres. The Pitch n' Putt golf course is 6 acres.

Wild vegetation other than trees.

It is possible to catalog every species of plant that grows wild at Green Lake, but since my interest was chiefly the trees, I did not do so. Because some people want to learn about these things, however, while walking around the lake's main path, I made notes of those plants and shrubs observed growing wild near the water's edge. Mushrooms, mosses and most grasses were excluded. Plants that only grow submerged in the water, such as the notorious Eurasian Water-Milfoil, were also ignored. With these exceptions, and some others missed because of their ephemeral nature or rarity, the following is what I found—54 kinds. Natives are marked **N**.

Vines and vinelike plants: 5 total; none native.

Blackberry, Cutleaf or Evergreen	*Rubus laciniatus*
Blackberry, Himalaya	*Rubus discolor*
Ivy, Common or English	*Hedera Helix*
Wild Morning Glory (Bindweed)	*Calystegia (Convolvulus) sepia*
Wild Morning Glory, Pink	*Calystegia sepia* f. *rosea*

Shrubs: 4 total; 2 native.

Broom, Scotch	*Cytisus scoparius*
Hardhack **N**	*Spiræa Douglasii* **N**
Red Osier **N**	*Cornus occidentalis* **N**
Rose	*Rosa* sp.

Grasses, rushes, sedges: 10 total; 5 native.

Barley, Foxtail	*Hordeum jubatum*
Bluegrass	*Poa annua*
Bulrush, Softstem N	*Scirpus validus* N
Cattail N	*Typha latifolia* N
Orchard Grass	*Dactylis glomerata*
Reed Canary Grass	*Phalaris arundinacea*
Rush, Common N	*Juncus effusus* N
Rush, Toad N	*Juncus bufonius* N
Sedge N	*Carex* sp. N
Velvet Grass	*Holcus lanatus*

Ferns and horsetails: 3; all native.

Bracken Fern N	*Pteridium aquilinum* N
Horsetail, Common N	*Equisteum arvense* N
Horsetail, Giant N	*Equisteum Telmateia* N

Floating and aquatic plants: 6 total; 3 native.

Duckweed N	*Lemna minor* N
Iris, Yellow	*Iris Pseudacorus*
Loosestrife, Purple	*Lythrum Salicaria*
Water Celery N	*Œnanthe sarmentosa* N
Water Lily N	*Nymphæa odorata* N
Water Pepper	*Polygonum Hydropiper*

Wildflowers, weeds, herbs: 26 total; 4 native.

Aster N	*Aster Eatonii* N
Burdock	*Arctium minus*
Buttercup, Creeping	*Ranunculus repens*
Cat's Ear	*Hypochæris radicata*
Chickweed	*Stellaria media*
Clover, Red	*Trifolium pratense*
Clover, White	*Trifolium repens*
Daisy, Lawn	*Bellis perennis*
Dandelion	*Taraxacum officinale*
Devil's Shoestring	*Polygonum aviculare*
Dock, Broad	*Rumex obtusifolius*
Dock, Curly	*Rumex crispus*
Fireweed, Common N	*Epilobium angustifolium* N
Fireweed, Dwarf N	*Epilobium ciliatum* N
Knotweed, Japanese	*Polygonum cuspidatum*
Lambsquarters	*Chenopodium album*
Mustard, Hedge	*Sisymbrium officinale*
Peppermint	*Mentha piperita*

Pineapple Weed N	*Matricaria matricarioides* N
Plantain, Broad	*Plantago major*
Plantain, English	*Plantago lanceolata*
Smartweed	*Polygonum Persicaria*
Thistle, Bull	*Cirsium vulgare*
Thistle, Canada	*Cirsium arvense*
Thistle, Sow	*Sonchus oleraceus*
Wormwood	*Artemisia Absinthium*

SEASONAL CHANGES: CALENDAR.

As Walden was to Thoreau, Green Lake is to Seattleites. We can learn its seasonal moods intimately by thoughtful observation of its natural history. By doing so, we find rest, fascination and inspiration. The lake's water mirrors whatever the variable sky is doing. The plant and animal life is even more changeable. What a difference there is between a sunny June day and an overcast, blustery November one! June can be fresh, floral, and full of smiling people warming themselves in the sun. November's cold wind can whip across the lake while screaming crows and the tracery of naked trees are silhouetted against dull gray skies. If great loads of snow come fast, deep and unexpectedly, even the otherwise ceaseless roar of Aurora is silenced.

Certain evergreen trees look quite similar regardless of when they are seen. Holly is a good example. But all trees have a period at which they are most becoming to human eyes. Holly reaches this point when laden with ripe berries in autumn and early winter. There are cherry trees worth looking at only while they're blooming. The following monthly calendar is designed to suggest the best times to see Green Lake trees.

January

January is the mirror image of December: instead of shivering through the slow journey *into* cold and dormancy, it is the opposite—the crawling infancy of spring.

TREES: a few ALDER catkins open late in the month if there is a warm spell; Whitcomb CHERRY can begin to bloom (bright pink); Cornelian-cherry DOGWOOD can bloom (yellow); Bigleaf MAPLE seedlings begin to sprout in late January; YEW can release pollen.

February

Winter's cold grip begins to yield noticeably to the warm embrace of spring. Woodland ravines and warm city back yards which receive some sun, and are protected from cold winds and frost, boast the earliest growth. The exposed lake is slower to flush forth signs of spring.

TREES: ALDER catkins; Incense CEDAR pollen; Whitcomb CHERRY continues (bright pink); Cornelian-cherry DOGWOOD continues (yellow); American ELM flowers (inconspicuous); Bigleaf MAPLE seedlings sprout; Cherry PLUM (white); Moseri PLUM (pink); Coast REDWOOD sheds pollen; YEW continues.

March

By late March *most* native deciduous shrubs and trees are leafing out. We still may have serious frosts, not to mention much rain, and sometimes sunshine or fog for variety's sake.

TREES: ALDER catkins continue; Orchard APPLES may begin blooming in late March (white); a few Bitter and Mazzard CHERRY may bloom in late March (white); Whitcomb CHERRY continues (bright pink), and regular Higan CHERRY blooms (pink); 'Shirotae' CHERRY (white); Yoshino CHERRY (white or pale pink); COTTONWOOD bud-scales fall all over, sticky and fragrant; Lawson CYPRESS releases pollen; Cornelian-cherry DOGWOOD continues (yellow); ELM blossoms (inconspicuous); Common HAWTHORN greens; HORNBEAM catkins; HORSE-CHESTNUT buds burst into leaf; LARCHES greening; Star MAGNOLIA begins flowering (white); Bigleaf MAPLE blooms (yellow); Bigleaf MAPLE seedlings continue to sprout; Chinese PHOTINIA unfolds its coppery young leaves; Moseri and Cherry PLUM continue, with 'Pissardii' (white or palest pink); Purple Pony PLUM (pink); Coast and Sierra REDWOOD release pollen; SERVICEBERRY begins blooming (white); TULIP TREES greening; Goldtwig WILLOW is spectacularly bright; Pussy-WILLOW buds out; YEW continues.

April

April is the month of general awakening, even though early risers bloomed in March and later stragglers come on in May. Dandelions color vast areas into seas of gold, while the chartreuse color of Bigleaf MAPLE blooms light up the forests. It is the last month of frost. Now the beauty of spring tempts us to sit back and enjoy, take long walks, sniff the flowers, etc. April is the prime cherry blossom month.

TREES: APPLES bloom; Crab-APPLES in late April (white or deep pink); BEECH (inconspicuous); Deodar CEDAR sheds cone debris, needles soon to follow; Bitter and Mazzard CHERRY continue (white); Kwanzan and the other Sato zakura CHERRIES (white, yellow or pink); Sour CHERRY hybrid (white); COTTONWOOD catkins; Pacific DOGWOOD (white); GINKGO can bloom late in the month (greenish-white); GOLDENCHAIN (yellow); Common HAWTHORN bloom (white) begins in late April; HOLLIES bloom (white, tiny); HORNBEAM catkins; HORSE-CHESTNUT in late April (white); Bigleaf MAPLE continues (yellow); Norway MAPLE blooms (yellow); Sycamore MAPLE blooms (yellow-green); Vine MAPLE blooms (red & white, tiny); MOUNTAIN-ASH (creamy white); OAKS bloom in late April (inconspicuous); Chinese PHOTINIA (white); PINE pollen; POPLAR catkins; SERVICEBERRY blooming (white); SWEETGUM can bloom in late April (inconspicuous); Pacific WILLOW catkins; Weeping WILLOW catkins in late April; White WILLOW catkins in late April.

May

Now the majority of trees are putting forth new foliage. The fresh rank growth of greens and flowers make the landscape rich. All the plants which had died down in winter now resurrect from their sleepy roots. It is the month of tent caterpillars.

TREES: APPLES can still be in bloom; Common BEECH continues blooming (inconspicuous); Red BUCKEYE (red); Yellow BUCKEYE (yellow); Bitter CHERRY continues (white); COTTONWOOD cotton; Pacific and Eastern DOGWOOD (white); ELM seeds everywhere; GINKGO continues (greenish-white, inconspicuous); GOLDENCHAIN continues (yellow); Autumn Glory, Cockspur, Common, HAWTHORNS bloom (all white); HOLLIES bloom (white, tiny); HORSE-CHESTNUT continues (white); Black LOCUST blooms (white); Bigleaf MAPLE still blooms in early May; MOUNTAIN-ASH (creamy white); Chinese PHOTINIA (white); Austrian Black and Shore PINE pollen; PLANE blooms (inconspicuous); White POPLAR cotton; TULIP TREE blooms (green and orange); ZELKOVA (inconspicuous).

June

June officially introduces summer with the longest day of the year. A plethora of flowers respond in grand fashion, and the entire month is an explosion of color. The freshness of spring is still present, the seediness of summer to come lies in the future. Fresh fruits are also ripening in mouth-watering amounts. Insects, too, seem to multiply madly, and aphids love to feast on plants limp with stress from the heavy warmth of the sudden sun. Butterflies and moths, spiders and others, make themselves felt in our lives.

TREES: Northern CATALPA blooms (white); COTTONWOOD cotton continues; Kousa DOGWOODS (white tinged with pink in age); Alpine GOLDENCHAIN (yellow); Cockspur HAWTHORN blooms (white); Black LOCUST continues (white); Evergreen MAGNOLIA (white); POPLAR cotton; SERVICEBERRIES ripening; Japanese SNOWBELL TREE (white).

July

July is our driest month, in terms of rainfall, but since June is often moist, August proves drier in a practical sense. June is often *spring* reluctantly being shown the exit, but July is summer. After the noise and smoke of the 4th, we settle into a very comfortable pattern of delightfully lengthy days, warm from beginning to end. The *rapidity* of plant growth now is immensely satisfying to green-thumbed humans. The heat brings forth amazing surges of vigor from certain vines and plants from continental climates. The first substantial loads of fruit begin to overwhelm us. We start to see *straw*-colored spring bulbs and meadows, and then lawns. We appreciate our shade trees.

TREES: CATALPA blooms (white); Mazzard CHERRIES are edible; Kousa DOGWOOD continues (white fading pink); GOLDEN RAIN TREE begins blooming yellow in late July; Evergreen MAGNOLIA continues (white); many MOUNTAIN ASH berries are bright red by late July; Cherry PLUM fruit is ready to eat; SILK TREE blooms (rosy); SORREL TREE blooms (white).

August

As August's scorching sun burns the grass of our lawns into the color of straw, we know the full might of summer is here. Many trees take on an unhealthy, yellowish, dull cast. Rain is rare. It is fascinating to observe which plants thrive even with no watering: natives generally do, as well as many weeds, and dozens of dry-climate exotics. The warm juice of fresh plums and peaches, the savor of beans and other green vegetables, make our diets now the healthiest of any season, though the heat may kill our appetite! Pounds of nature's purest offerings rot on the ground, left by people too busy to gather and preserve; our compost heaps swell with the fruit of the earth.

TREES: APPLES ripe; BEECHnuts ripening this month; Southern CATALPA can continue to bloom (white); last of the Mazzard CHERRIES to eat in early August; native Pacific DOGWOODS begin their second bloom (white) as their bitter but pretty orange-red berries ripen; Cornelian-Cherry DOGWOOD berries are edible late in August; the first FIGS are ready to eat; FIR cones are now conspicuous; GOLDEN RAIN TREE continues (yellow); MOUNTAIN ASH berries are brightly orange-colored; the earliest OAK acorns ripen; SILK TREE continues (rosy); YEW berries redden.

September

If the color of August is yellow, September is russet. Rains return, temperatures cool—much to our comfort; the leaves of some trees start to color and fall. Later in the month, fog frequently makes cold, wet mornings, but then is burnt away by afternoon sun. The weather, in a word, is *ideal* for outdoor activity; the shorter days start to annoy us! It is a safe period to go vacationing without dreading that everything will collapse in your absence. Children may hate September, for its back-to-school blues.

TREES: APPLES; Redvein Crab-APPLE can have some flowers; BEECHnuts; Atlas CEDAR pollen; Western Red CEDAR old parts are dropping; Bitter CHERRY fruit ripe; Cornelian-Cherry DOGWOOD berries edible; Eastern, Kousa and Pacific DOGWOOD fruits showy red, some flowers (white) still on our native; FIGS edible; GOLDEN RAIN TREE continues (yellow); Common HAWTHORN berries red; HORSE-CHESTNUT nuts ready for squirrels; MOUNTAIN ASHES lovely with berries; OAK acorns; White PINE needles are dropping; Coast and Sierra REDWOOD needles are dropping; SILK TREE continues (rosy); Black WALNUTS begin to be ready for gathering; WITCH-HAZEL blooms (yellow, tiny); YEW berries turn red.

October

October starts as leftover summer and ends in autumn at its peak. The fog gradually gives way to light frosts, kissing a cold goodbye to summer annuals and tender perennials. Compared to September there are fewer flowers, but more *color*, because although many summer fruits are totally depleted, new fall fruits such as grapes don their colorful garb of ripeness, and of course there are the bright leaves of trees and many shrubs. The long, dry, golden grass of summer now begins to give way to refreshing greenery at the soil line, and rainfall means mushrooms are among us.

TREES: APPLES edible; Crab-APPLE fruit can be showy, especially 'Red Jewell'; burgundy-colored Caucasian ASH; BEECH turns rusty gold; BEECHnuts edible; BIRCHES are yellow; Yellow BUCKEYE is orange; Deodar CEDAR cones are showy, and the male catkins shed their pollen; Western Red CEDAR sheds old foliage; Bitter CHERRY yellows or is bare though Mazzard CHERRIES are just beginning to color; sometimes there is still Cornelian-cherry DOGWOOD fruit to eat; some flowers remain on the native Pacific DOGWOOD; Kousa DOGWOOD berries are plump; American ELMS yellowing; FIGS edible; GINKGO is yellowing, with orange fruit on the females; Cockspur HAWTHORN showy with red fruit; HOLLY berries showy; HORSE-CHESTNUTS yellow brown, their inedible nuts on the ground; Bigleaf MAPLE colors the landscape gold or tawny; some MOUNTAIN ASHES are crimson; OAK acorns fall; Pin OAKS are red; the pink-purple of White OAK is lovely; SERVICEBERRY is red; SORREL TREE is crimson; SWEETGUMS in part are colorful, mostly red but some still green; TULIP TREE is yellow; WALNUTS edible, as the leaves turn yellow; WITCH-HAZEL continues blooming (yellow, tiny); YEW berries are red; ZELKOVA is yellow to rusty-red; REDWOODS, PINES and CEDARS continue to drop old foliage.

November

Bright fall color early in the month is warm to behold, but light frosts usually grow serious; leaf collection becomes a dripping, heavy chore. The days are mercilessly short. Snow is possible. Some of our most ferocious windstorms, and great flooding, has occurred in November. There is wide variation yearly, with the mild years and hard ones contrasting totally. The key is *when* the killer frost arrives in *force*, if it does at all. It is our *mild* winters that set us apart from the ice-land east of the Cascades. Warm places in the city, especially, have an almost frost-free micro-climate, even though 10 miles away in the country, great sheets of white frost cover browned vegetation.

(**November** *continued*)
TREES: ALDERS drop their leaves green; APPLES are still edible; ASPEN is yellow; Deodar CEDAR sheds pollen; Mazzard CHERRY yellow or red; COTTONWOOD yellow; Bald CYPRESS is bronzy-purple; possibly still some Cornelian-Cherry DOGWOOD fruit edible early in the month; Hybrid and Smoothleaf ELMS dull yellow; Douglas FIR sheds old needles; GINKGO is yellow; Autumn Glory HAWTHORN fruit is worth looking at; HORNBEAM is yellow; Japanese MAPLES colorful; Norway MAPLE yellow; Lombardy POPLAR yellow; Dawn REDWOOD red brown; SWEETGUM can be any color; TULIPTREE yellow-gold; Black WALNUTS still edible; WITCH-HAZEL continues blooming (yellow, tiny); YEW berries persist.

December

Now it is real winter, with steamy breathing and icy streets. Still, it is unlike what *most* North Americans experience. Some stubborn *deciduous* trees and shrubs persistently hold their leaves as if trying to prove something. Nonetheless, with the sun so low on the horizon, and the days so short, nobody is really fooled.

TREES: ALDER and BIRCH seeds are falling; Red Jewell Crab-APPLE fruit is showy; HOLLY berries are brilliant; the last trees to drop their leaves are certain Black COTTONWOODS, Bald CYPRESSES, GOLDENCHAINS, LARCHES, SILK TREES, SWEETGUMS, WILLOWS.

TOURING GREEN LAKE'S TREES

These notes will enable you to walk around the lake with an eye for trees not missing any rare or outstanding examples. The park is divided into eight sections, and the most notable trees of each area are indicated. To appreciate the park's trees fully, you must often walk on the lawn areas; staying on the paved lakeside path will force you to miss some major trees.

East area—fieldhouse, pool, parking-lot, ballfields.

Double rows of Hybrid PLANETREES east of the fieldhouse / Evans Pool building lend landmark status to the park's most heavily used area, and divide it: south of the PLANES are ballfields; northward are tennis courts, a concession, a children's area, and a parking lot. Most of the trees around the ballfield portion are average examples of BIRCHES, HAWTHORNS and MAPLES. Only the 'Schwedler' Norway MAPLE is special. However, on the mounds towards Ravenna Boulevard are three kinds of trees not found elsewhere at Green Lake: nine BEECHES, one Bitter CHERRY, and four Moser Purpleleaf PLUMS. This vicinity also has the largest Austrian Black PINE, and is well stocked with CHERRIES worth admiring in April: Kwanzan, Mazzard, Temari, Ukon, Yoshino—and to the north (with five Norway SPRUCES) is Shiro-fugen. The park's two best Oriental ARBORVITÆS are at the east end of the PLANETREE row.

The building's walls and patio have some trees not present elsewhere: six Pyramidal ARBORVITÆS, seven Leyland CYPRESSES, one pink-flowering Eastern DOGWOOD, one purpleleaf Japanese MAPLE, one Chinese PHOTINIA. The small Shirotae or Mt. Fuji CHERRIES at the corners are rare at the park.

Southwest of the building, on the beach, is the park's only Hybrid ELM, south of a much smaller Smoothleaf ELM, which in turn is south of the only White POPLAR. On the beach west and northwest of the building are a HORSE-CHESTNUT, two gnarly Black LOCUSTS, and 11 ZELKOVAS. North of the building is the lone Whitcomb CHERRY, a four-trunked Mountain PINE, and a large, grassy traffic island stocked with two White FIRS, three Pin OAKS, five Evergreen MAGNOLIAS and a Japanese SNOWBELL TREE.

The children's play area mound supports the park's only Double-flowering European Crab-APPLE. Not far away is the unique Paul's Scarlet HAWTHORN, beyond which are three GINKGOS. The pair of dark, tall Weeping Lawson CYPRESSES are exceedingly rare. Moving beyond the play area to the grassy expanse, there are numerous trees which are common at the park, the only notable ones being the blue Lawson CYPRESSES and two impressively large Atlas CEDARS.

Northeast shore—Bald Cypress territory.

Cross the entrance road lined by TULIP TREES, stay east of the tennis courts, and you will be in a grove of skinny, mixed conifers. In their scrawny multitude, compare the 14 Sawara CYPRESSES with their four Plume and three Moss varieties. Disregard the MOUNTAIN ASHES—better ones come later. Round the corner of the tennis courts and behold the tallest Bald CYPRESS grove, and first Red HAWTHORN. Nearby are Weeping POPLARS, and three Sierra REDWOODS. Over near the road are six Sawara CYPRESSES with the park's best Western Red CEDAR.

Approaching Sunnyside Avenue, note three leaning Atlas CEDARS next to two European LARCHES; the park's best Caucasian FIR, right next to a smaller green Colorado SPRUCE. At Sunnyside Avenue are three Zebra CEDARS. Just beyond Sunnyside is the park's largest Yoshino CHERRY. In the vicinity are plenty of Higan and Kwanzan CHERRIES for comparison. Opposite Corliss are two more very big Yoshino CHERRIES.

Beyond Bagley Avenue, opposite house #7556 is a Greek FIR, west of two Douglas FIRS. With ten Bald CYPRESSES are five Eastern DOGWOODS. The first Cockspur HAWTHORN is hereabouts (so much more handsome than the twiggy Red HAWTHORNS). By the water is a Goldtwig WILLOW.

Opposite Meridian Avenue, with three Bald CYPRESSES, is a big-berried MOUNTAIN ASH. Just beyond is a bench commemorating Maury Hagen, Junior, with nearby SERVICEBERRY, FIG and SORREL TREE. Gaines Point has 28 landmark COTTONWOODS.

Beyond Orin Court, near the water are two smaller big-berried MOUNTAIN ASHES with two yucchy Red HAWTHORNS. Towards the street is a Golden Sawara CYPRESS, three regular Sawaras and two Threadleafs. With a grove of ten Bald CYPRESSES is another fair Threadleaf Sawara CYPRESS. Near the lake is the first Ringleaf WILLOW.

The caretaker's building by 77th has various interesting trees around it. On the street side is a Purple Pony purpleleaf PLUM. Two Globe or round-headed Black LOCUSTS are present. Eight 'Allumii' or Scarab Lawson CYPRESSES are scattered about. A five-foot tall Noble FIR (*Abies procera*) was planted between the lake and the building in late February 1992, right before this book went to press, but is so damaged that it may die rather than become a new park ornament.

North tip—wading pool and vicinity.

Beyond the caretaker's building by 77th, near the water is an excellent Ringleaf WILLOW (pictured on this book's cover). By the road are two Golden Sawara CYPRESSES with three smaller Thread Sawara CYPRESSES and two Lawson CYPRESSES. Closer towards 78th Street are the first of the muddy Purple Crab-APPLES. The COTTONWOODS found here are bigger than those seen earlier.

By the north restrooms are eleven PLANES. Across the asphalt path, nearer the wading pool, is one tiny Siberian ELM, a Downy BIRCH by a bigger White BIRCH, four small Red HAWTHORNS, seven Bald CYPRESSES. North of the wading pool is a crowded grove, the only trees *rare* at the park being the four English YEWS, two tiny Kousa DOGWOODS, and the English MAPLE. Northwest of the wading pool is a magnificent Sycamore MAPLE—the park's largest. Near it are two Cockspur HAWTHORNS and two Higan CHERRIES. Less close to the road are two Paper BIRCHES, one being Green Lake's largest.

Back by the wading pool's outlet steam, near the stone footbridge, are two pines. One (tall and slender) is the park's only Red PINE (North American Red Pine, anyway; *Japanese* Red Pines are common); the other (squat, limby specimen), by the lake, is an Austrian Black PINE.

The ten giant Sierra REDWOODS are monumental evergreen landmarks, the largest trunk being 20 feet around. Also here are the park's finest Deodar CEDARS. On the south side of the major path that connects to 77th Street, is a heart-shaped planting bed with the two tiny Cornelian-Cherry DOGWOODS and an Eastern DOGWOOD. Not far away is another young planting: a Star MAGNOLIA and a White FIR, the latter doomed from too much shade cast by the mature Sawara CYPRESSES and Zebra CEDARS.

Along the road now begin Norway MAPLE street-trees. By the lake are two Ringleaf WILLOWS, ALDERS, and ten Eastern DOGWOODS.

Northwest area—the trees at their best.

As you head south towards 76th Street, there is a bench with a young SWEETGUM tree. Up near the road is the giant Norway MAPLE. The lakeside is dark with ALDERS, COTTONWOODS and WILLOWS.

Opposite 76th Street is a Horinji CHERRY suffering under two European LARCHES; nearby is the first Oriental SPRUCE as well as a Yoshino CHERRY. Nearer the lake are some Scots PINES with ALDERS and the last Ringleaf WILLOW. Three prominent Atlas CEDARS cannot be overlooked. South of them is a row that has six Oriental SPRUCES, three Japanese Red PINES, three Lawson CYPRESSES, two Sycamore MAPLES, one Himalayan White PINE hybrid and one Chinese PINE; there are also three towering Lombardy POPLARS.

The Bathhouse Theatre walls have three Pissard Purpleleaf PLUMS and one burly-trunked greenleaf Cherry PLUM. Shrubby HOLLIES and Portugal LAUREL (*Prunus lusitanica*) are also present.

West of the theatre is a large bed that contains one young Red Jewell™ Crab-APPLE, one Horinji CHERRY, one Mikuruma-gaeshi CHERRY, one Naden CHERRY, one Ojochin CHERRY, two pink Oshima CHERRIES, one white Oshima CHERRY, two Shirotae or Mount Fuji CHERRIES, one Ukon CHERRY, six GOLDENCHAINS, five Alpine GOLDENCHAINS, three WITCH-HAZELS. As if that wasn't enough, west and south of the bed are Kwanzan CHERRIES, some quite enormous. So here is an excellent place to learn flowering cherry varieties.

Elm Hill is across the path southwest of the theatre. It has two Western Red CEDARS with five Norway SPRUCES, three Norway MAPLES, one curiously *split* Sycamore MAPLE on the highest point of ground, four American White ELMS and one Smoothleaf ELM.

The parking lot's long, narrow bed has seven Kwanzan CHERRIES, one Temari CHERRY, one Ukon CHERRY, nine GOLDEN RAIN trees, and a young Eastern DOGWOOD. The shrubs include *Spiræa, Forsythia, Weigela, Viburnum plicatum*, and azaleas.

Going back from the parking lot towards the lake, there is a path that skirts Elm Hill. This path goes by the park's four largest GOLDEN RAIN TREES, with HOLLIES, four GOLDENCHAINS, three Colorado SPRUCES, and a WITCH-HAZEL. Just beyond, out in the grassy area, is a Kwanzan CHERRY next to the park's only Sour CHERRY hybrid. Proceed on the path to the huge boulder. This rock once had a plaque, which most likely told how the ELMS and crab-APPLES had been planted in 1932 to commemorate the bicentennial of the birth of George Washington. Seven Redvein or Turkestan Crab-APPLES line the main lake path here.

Head back onto the lawn towards the whitebarked BIRCHES. It appears there are two White BIRCHES, one Downy BIRCH, and one *hybrid* between the two species! Distinguishing them is a pain. Beyond them, overlooking the parking lot again, is a grove of six Japanese and two European LARCHES. Though the Europeans are common at Green Lake, this is the only planting of the Asian species, so now is the time to compare them.

Climb onto Oak Hill and observe three Bur OAKS, two Pin OAKS, four Red OAKS and four Scarlet OAKS. Back down towards the lake, the path is lined with nine runty Siberian Crab-APPLES and two larger Kaido or Midget Crab-APPLES at the row's end. On the lake side of the path you will find (if it is still standing) the park's largest ALDER, about 90 feet tall with its trunk more than 9 feet around. Plenty of smaller ones are nearby.

Continue on the broad flat grassy area towards the conifer grove near where people feed birds (a practice now being discouraged). This grove is a beautiful bit of shadowy woodland to walk through, containing: ten Japanese Red PINES, 16 Eastern White PINES and six Veitch FIRS. The main path between this evergreen grove and Oak Hill, has six Kaido or Midget Crab-APPLES, with a much larger Purple Crab-APPLE.

Head for the parking lot and on your right are nine Sitka SPRUCES, in front of 16 Downy BIRCHES with two White BIRCHES. On your left are eleven Redvein or Turkestan Crab-APPLES.

The northwest tennis courts are surrounded by conifers. On the street side are 6 CEDARS of Lebanon, five Eastern White PINES and a Norway MAPLE. Round the corner by the COTTONWOODS and there are eight Japanese Red PINES, 8 Eastern White PINES and three Veitch FIRS. Now, on the lake side of the courts are 12 Scots PINES, seven Chinese PINES and six Japanese Red PINES, plus an ALDER and some lovable broad *bushes* that have riotous neon red fall color: *Euonymus alatus*, the Winged Spindletree.

Proceed towards a huge conifer grove, containing 11 Norway SPRUCES, 11 Japanese Red PINES, nine Eastern White PINES, six white FIRS and three Veitch FIRS. New, over by the street, is the only specimen of Autumn Glory HAWTHORN. Some of the very largest COTTONWOODS are in this area.

Western strip—by busy Aurora.

This segment is narrow, noisy and not well diversified with trees. Going from north to south, it begins with many PINES. 21 Scots PINES, 12 Japanese Red PINES, two Eastern White PINES. By the water you can see a small, three-trunked male Pacific Black WILLOW, healthier Goldtwig WILLOWS, two COTTONWOODS, and an ALDER.

Southward beyond 71st Street is an Atlas CEDAR, 14 Japanese Red PINES, ten Chinese PINES and three Eastern White PINES. Additional Scots PINES, the Shore PINES, and SILK TREES are found next, plus more of the same common trees you have been seeing. South of 70th, by the water, are Goldtwig WILLOWS, two young Quaking ASPENS, Sitka Pussy WILLOWS, Sepulchral WILLOWS, ALDERS, COTTONWOODS, and south of 68th is a grove of seven Bald CYPRESSES.

South of 67th Street are four Siberian ELMS, with ALDERS, bushy Shore PINES and Bigleaf MAPLES.

Next to the water are three shrubby Pacific Black WILLOWS, with a Goldtwig WILLOW south of them. South of 66th Street is a spidery Atlas CEDAR near Kwanzan CHERRIES, Japanese Red PINES and two Douglas FIRS.

Opposite 65th Street is a Corkscrew WILLOW. Above it, on the grass, are Shore PINES.

Southwest—strip below Woodland Park.

Numerous *young* trees are found here. Namely, 35 Douglas FIRS, 18 Incense CEDARS, 13 SWEETGUMS, 13 Norway MAPLES edging the parking lot, seven Red OAKS, and two SORREL TREES. Along the road are the Black WALNUTS planted in 1919 as a memorial to Seattle soldiers killed in the first world war. Five young HORSE-CHESTNUTS are also with them. By the water are huge, hideous Pacific Black WILLOWS and a second Corkscrew WILLOW. Just beyond the north tip of the parking lot, a fascinating Southern CATALPA is one of the larger, older trees.

South—Aqua Theatre and Pitch n' Putt vicinity.

Not far from the restrooms are some old, large trees. Most notable is the huge Hybrid PLANE, differing from the three other PLANES south of it. A TULIP TREE is here, also.

Behind the Small Craft Center are seven bushy Kousa DOGWOODS, and eight young Austrian Black PINES crowded together. Four large Atlas CEDARS are by the cars. Four more Kousa DOGWOODS are with rhododendrons. The park's only Hinoki CYPRESSES are two small ones in a bed that also has a much larger plume Sawara CYPRESS and a young SORREL TREE.

Between the Pitch n' Putt golf course and the parking lot is a stretch full of trees, some of them wild. Highlights include: Norway MAPLES, two slender Pacific DOGWOODS by a small boulder, and six Mazzard CHERRIES. Nearby is a green *and* a bluish Colorado SPRUCE with a Deodar CEDAR.

East of the Aqua Theatre are six Ponderosa PINES, three Scots PINES, three Dawn REDWOODS, a very blue Colorado SPRUCE near the dock, three Caucasian FIRS and one Greek FIR.

An amazing OAK collection is on both sides of the path north of the Pitch n' Putt golf course. On the water or north side of the path is a Swamp White OAK, then a smaller Black OAK, then a much smaller Bur OAK. On the golf course side of the path, is an Oriental White OAK, then a huge Daimyo OAK, then a small Oriental White OAK, then a big White OAK hybrid, and, last, a White OAK.

In the Pitch n' Putt golf course itself are some special trees. To see them, you can buy a game of golf, or peek over the fence. Or, *in winter* when no golf is played, you can stroll around without bothering anyone, except Canada geese who think they own the place. Species appearing *only* in the golf course are two decrepit White WILLOW hybrids, one HORNBEAM, two Orchard APPLES, three greenleaved Japanese MAPLES, six Coast REDWOODS, two young Vine MAPLES, and three young Rocky Mountain JUNIPERS. Species in the golf course that are the largest of their kind at Green Lake are Douglas FIR, Mugo PINE, European LARCH and TULIP TREE.

Between the golf course and the lake is a willow thicket. Most are Goldtwig WILLOWS, many are Pacific Black WILLOWS, there may be a few Pussy WILLOWS, there is at least one Sepulchral WILLOW, and one White WILLOW, the latter not far from a whitebarked birch tree.

Northeast of the golf course are Incense CEDARS, Douglas FIRS, Norway and Sycamore MAPLES, and the park's only Red HORSE-CHESTNUT and only Yellow BUCKEYE. The park's only four Japanese Black PINES are accompanied by two much younger Austrian Black PINES.

Southeast—narrow strip with few trees.

Going from the golf course toward Kenwood Place, there is a SILK TREE, 13 Sycamore MAPLES, two Norway MAPLES, two MOUNTAIN ASHES, and two GOLDENCHAIN trees. Near the water is a Sepulchral WILLOW, north of it a Weeping White BIRCH. Moving northward towards Kirkwood Place are many more of the same common trees, plus eight HAWTHORNS, two Kwanzan CHERRIES, and three ALDERS. Opposite Kirkwood Place is the champion Veitch FIR, plus a smaller associate, and a Douglas FIR; and a Kwanzan CHERRY and a Paper BIRCH.

North of Kirkwood Place are three LARCHES and a leaning, two-trunked Black LOCUST, then a Paper BIRCH and a one each of a Higan and Kwanzan CHERRY. Near the water in this area are an ugly Goldtwig WILLOW, COTTONWOODS, a Paper BIRCH, and a multitrunked ALDER.

Opposite 63rd Street are five Douglas FIRS and two Veitch FIRS. Northward are 8 Zebra CEDARS by the lake. Around the giant Sepulchral WILLOW are five tall LARCHES, a Sycamore MAPLE and two Bigleaf MAPLES.

By the water opposite the restrooms, are six White BIRCHES with one Downy BIRCH. The park's biggest Bigleaf MAPLE is by the restrooms, with six others, and two Sycamore MAPLES. Northward are more BIRCHES, young COTTONWOODS, and WILLOWS near the water.

By 65th Street are 3 Norway MAPLES, three Bigleaf MAPLES and two Sycamore MAPLES. In front of these are two young White FIRS and a Star MAGNOLIA planted in 1991 (plus—possibly—three pussy WILLOWS that grew from twigs someone stuck in during late February, 1992). Northward is an Oriental SPRUCE, a Kwanzan CHERRY, and two Alpine GOLDENCHAINS.

Opposite 67th Street stand two Norway MAPLES, and six Sycamore MAPLES (including the wineleaf variety). Opposite them by the lake, is a Weeping White BIRCH.

The final leg, between 67th and Sunnyside, has many White BIRCHES by the water, some being the weeping variety. On higher ground are the park's eight bushy Tanyosho PINES; a Sierra REDWOOD; two SILK TREES; the largest Oriental SPRUCE; one Yoshino with two Kwanzan CHERRIES; an Austrian Black PINE of good looks, that children enjoy climbing; a greenish Atlas CEDAR; a lopsided, torn American White ELM; two dying native Pacific DOGWOODS next to a female English YEW; two Southern CATALPAS (west of bench) and one Northern CATALPA (east of bench). The conifer grove by the YEW has seven plume Sawara CYPRESSES, one regular Sawara CYPRESS and one Oriental ARBORVITÆ. A second grove of evergreens, near the CATALPAS, has six moss Sawara CYPRESSES, four plume Sawara CYPRESSES, one regular Sawara CYPRESS, and one Zebra CEDAR.

Red ALDER
Alnus rubra

ALDER is like a dishrag—indispensable, but no thing of beauty. In a weird way, it almost compels a grudging admiration from us: for it carries plainness of appearance to the level of a high art. Every time such sentiments are expressed, some offended friend of alder rebukes me, insisting how enchantingly lovely a grove of these trees is, when their ghostly pale trunks are clothed in lichens, and the sunlight dances upon their slender, swaying shafts. Agreed. But, when planted as isolated specimen ornamental shade trees, red alders are *plain*. Their leaden green color is not even relieved by the time the leaves drop in November. Their cones are knobby, dark and more of a visual distraction than an asset. The dangling catkins of spring are, accompanied by the tender new greenery, not uninteresting per se, but are overshadowed by the flashy decorations of numerous other trees. Clearly, as far as looks are concerned, this tree excites no admiration.

Nonetheless, people see beyond beauty. Many trees are lovely to behold, but otherwise quite useless. Not so with alder. It is an ecologic heavyweight. Nature is never long bare of trees if alder has its way. Fast and thick it greens the open clearings, enriching the soil with nitrogen from its fallen leaves. It also produces a hardwood prized for many uses. Since this native species is so abundant, all of us who cherish familiarity with natural history, are already, or should become, intimately appreciative of the tree. Just—plant a gorgeous tree in your front yard; let alder stay wild.

Green Lake has over eighty alders, coming up wild around the edge. Most are on the west side, associated with willows, but easily distinguished by their coarse, wide leaves, and by bearing *cones* unlike most non-coniferous trees. The largest is about 90 feet tall, its trunk 9⅓ feet around, south of the Bathhouse Theatre.

33

Orchard APPLE
Malus domestica

TWO old apple trees of surpassing size are the star attractions at the southwest corner of Green Lake's Pitch n' Putt golf course, their origin wrapped in mystery—but they're certainly not the sort of trees normally seen in formally designed parks. Did a local Johnny Appleseed have a hand here? Probably they came up as seedlings in fill dirt dumped in 1932. In any case, these thriving giants offer a perfect example of how stimulating and impressive old, unpruned apple trees can be. Finding unpruned apple trees of such age and stature in the city is difficult, so cherish them, especially when they're blooming in May, or in winter when their sheer size is forceful to an unexpected degree.

The northernmost tree produces yellow fruit, somewhat red-blushed, 2 inches long, peculiarly narrow—looking like yellow eggs hanging on the branches after the leaves fall. Probably this tree is a *hybrid* between Seattle's native crab-apple (*Malus fusca*, not present at Green Lake) and an Orchard Apple.

Crab APPLES in general.

MORE than 170 different crab-apple varieties are for sale in North American nurseries. Such stupendous diversity is unheard of in other ornamental trees—except the maples. In April or May, deliciously lovely flowers in generous abundance serve as a symbol of springtime promise, full of vigor and charm. Then, alas, on most varieties west of the Cascades, *scab* descends like a plague to spoil the trees. Petals wither with brown blotches, leaves dry, curl up and drop early. The fruit yield is reduced, and those that remain are often blighted. Three of Green Lake's six crabs suffer terribly from this fungus disease, and the others are not immune to its dreadful ravages. Only fungicide spraying each spring can combat the scab. It is much better to replace susceptible trees with disease-resistant kinds, which are every bit as handsome if not more so, in addition to being healthy. Crab-apple fruit is edible but not good usually—*some* varieties produce fruit as tasty as any regular apples.

Green Lake's original crab plantings resulted from the gift of 100 trees from the Seattle Garden Club in 1931.

Double-flowered European Crab-APPLE
Malus sylvestris 'Plena'

THIS is the rarest of Green Lake's crabs. In Europe, the wild crab is common, and indeed was the tree originally called "Crab Apple." It is of small, crooked form, bearing broad, blunt, thick, downy, veiny leaves that stay green into November. Its fruit is either yellowish with a bit of red blush, like a small orchard apple on a stout stalk, or sometimes is a mere greenish, hard little marble. Its flowers are charming: pinkish buds opening white. In the *double flowered* version, the 1½" flowers bear not only the customary five petals, but 13–15, thereby yielding a fuller, fluffier display that lasts longer. Dense clusters totally cover the tree. This variety is rare, and not found at nurseries. Green Lake's only specimen is on the mound at the children's play area northeast of the Evans Pool building. It blooms later than the other Green Lake crabs.

Kaido or Midget Crab-APPLE
Malus × *micromalus*

A Siberian crab hybrid from China and Japan, the Kaido Crab was introduced to the West about 1856. Its early flowers, from carmine buds, open palest pink, and are very attractive. Drink deep of their beauty. The leaves are long, slender and dark green. The fruit is ½–⅞" wide, green for ever so long, then finally plain yellow, all too quickly rotting to butterscotch brown.

Green Lake has two with the row of nine dwarfish Siberian crabs, plus six in a row by themselves still farther southwest of the Bathhouse Theatre. They are scabby, but less so than the nearby redvein, Siberian and purple crabs. [There is some doubt about the correctness of the identity I've assigned this tree. Most books say the fruit is *red*. But the crab-apple labeled *Malus* × *micromalus* at Seattle's arboretum, is like these Green Lake trees.]

Purple Crab-APPLE
Malus × *purpurea*

ONE of the numerous offspring of the redvein crab, this originated around 1900 at a famous French nursery, Barbier's of Orléans. Compared to redvein crab, it is a darker, denser, glossier tree. Its flowers are smaller (1–1½" wide), darker (magenta), less fragrant, and borne on elegant long stalks. The leaves are narrower, sleeker, more sharply toothed, and are sometimes a bit *lobed* on strong sucker shoots. The fruit is more like what we expect in a crab: hard, dark reddish, cherry-sized affairs ¾–1" long.

Like the redvein crab, this tree is scab-prone, therefore repulsive to look at, and is fortunately no longer offered in the nursery trade. Old specimens exist more than 40 feet tall and wide. When pruned, sprayed, and seen only during full bloom, they are an arresting spectacle. But when left alone, unsprayed, and seen in the summer, the Purple Crab should be arrested for indecent exposure. Judge for yourself—I think they are the ugliest trees at Green Lake.

There are 22, chiefly east of the wading pool—with a lone giant by the row of kaido crabs not far east of the northwest tennis courts.

Red Jewell™ Crab-APPLE
Malus Red Jewell™

THIS is prized for pure white flowers and pea-sized red berries. Red Jewell was introduced by the Cole Nursery, formerly of Painesville, Ohio, and is patented #3267; its name is trademarked. Why "jewel" was spelled with an additional "l" is a mystery, unless there was a connection with the Jewell Nursery of Lake City, Minnesota (established in 1868 and still in business).

In the nursery trade since 1972, Red Jewell Crab has remained in high repute consistently and deservedly. It is comparatively scabfree. This fact, plus its especially long-lasting attractive fruit make it one of the best crab-apple choices for our region. The tree grows broad and low. Its leaves are deep green, persistently hairy on both sides, and are sometimes lobed. The flowers are small (an inch or less wide), white from pink buds, with widely spaced petals. Numerous clusters of shiny red fruit, $\frac{3}{8}$" or larger on 1½ inch stalks, are showy and persistent in fall and winter. These are the red jewels.

Green Lake has but two, youngsters planted in 1990: one in the bed of flowering cherries, goldenchains and witch-hazels west of the Bathhouse Theatre (it stands about opposite of the theatres's rainbow-colored sign); the other near the office in the Pitch n' Putt golf course.

Redvein or Turkestan Crab-APPLE
Malus Niedzwetzkyana

THIS tree's tongue-twisting scientific name immortalizes the memory of Mr. Niedzwetzky, who introduced it to Europeans from its native lands of the Caucasus, southwest Siberia, and western China, more than 100 years ago.

Rich pigmentation is its soul. Or, to some of us: murky darkness is its drawback. The flowers are 1½–2" wide, and solid heavy purplish-pink; the unfolding leaves reveal reddish color beneath their silvery hairs; and the fruit is intensely dark, maroon on the outside, and a surprising red *inside*, too.

For several reasons the Redvein Crab is no longer sold at nurseries. Its fruits are not abundant, showy, or good to eat, but are so large (over 2" long frequently) as to make a bothersome mess. The tree is disgustingly susceptible to scab disease. Most importantly, we are indebted to the Redvein Crab for most of the dozens of better-looking "rosybloom" crab-apple varieties which stand out because of their strikingly purplish young leaves, deeply colored petals and dark-fleshed fruits. It is fascinating how the offspring are sometimes *darker* than their parent. In one word, the Redvein Crab has been superseded.

Green Lake has 20, from the northwest parking lot to the north restrooms. They could only be confused with the purple crab (page 36). There are 17 *sprayed* specimens at the U.W. near MacKenzie Hall, in case you care to see the trees in presentable condition. Curiously, Redvein Crabs sometimes bear a few clusters of flowers in September.

Siberian Crab-APPLE
Malus baccata

HERE is the crab-apple king—a title it earns by being ultra-hardy, earliest to blossom, unequaled in fecundity, and by spanning the breadth of Asia. Also, it grows about as large as any kind of crab. A variable species, it differs in details, but generally bears white, fragrant flowers earliest of all; the leaves are green, narrow and edged with fine sharp teeth; and the fruit are about blueberry size, though (usually) longer than broad; hard, shiny, and colored variously yellow (as at Green Lake), orange or red, borne on slender stems an inch and a half long.

Green Lake has nine in a row flanking the asphalt path by Oak Hill (southwest of the Bathhouse Theatre). They are, as usual, pitifully scabby, and set few fruit most years. Dwarfish in size, congested, it is difficult to admire them except when they are in bloom: dark red buds open white, 1⅓" wide. At the end of the row are two larger kaido crabs; redvein crabs are also nearby.

Oriental ARBORVITÆ
Thuja orientalis

TREES, like clothing styles, can be fashionable for some time, then lose their appeal to people. Oriental Arborvitæ no longer enjoys the popularity it once reveled in. Look at one of Green Lake's six specimens and you will instantly understand why the tree has come to be passed over. A coniferous evergreen, its foliage is dense, weakly fragrant, held in rigidly conventional upright sprays like books on a shelf, and its cones are pistachio-sized, plump, conspicuously pale bluish before ripening.

Although this Arborvitæ is a tree in its native lands of China, Burma and Korea, most that are cultivated in the U.S. are shrubby, or floppy small trees.

Green Lake's best example stood 26 feet tall before it had its top removed to accommodate overhead electric lines. It is south of the restrooms west of NE 72nd Street. A decapitated partner is nearby; four more elsewhere are not as attractive or large as these two. Three of the four are by the children's play area; the other grows north of an English yew northwest of where Sunnyside Avenue intersects Green Lake Way.

Pyramidal ARBORVITÆ
Thuja occidentalis 'Fastigiata'

SIX young Pyramidal Arborvitæs flank the walls of the fieldhouse/pool building. Presently they are more accent shrubs than trees, but in years to come they may attain 30 feet in height and be comparatively commanding. Pyramidal Arborvitæ is an abundantly planted columnar evergreen—some people will insist it's *too*-abundantly planted. Closely related to Seattle's native western red cedar, "Pyramidalis" (as it is known in the nursery trade) owes its ubiquity to its *tight narrowness*, excellent for screening or as a vertical accent. The ordinary Arborvitæ, on the other hand, also called Northern White Cedar, grows rather wide, and is not markedly dense. *Arbor Vitæ* means Tree of Life in Latin, because 16th century French sailors were saved from a dreadful scurvy fate in the wilderness by the life-preserving qualities of this tree—a tea of it gave the sailors vitamin C. Its sprays of resinous, scaly, compressed foliage earned the tree an old nickname: *Flat* Cedar.

Caucasian or Narrowleaf ASH
Fraxinus oxycarpa

GREEN LAKE'S only Caucasian or Narrowleaf Ash was planted in memory of "Dad." A pad of concrete ringing the 1990 planting is inscribed cryptically "R. W. Bayne. '25–'90" The tree is either the 'Raywood' or 'Flame' variety, two similar sorts, both distinguished by exquisite purplish fall color unlike regular seedlings of this species that manage merely to turn an average yellow in autumn. This species of the eastern Mediterranean and Caucasus Mountains (hence its name) is remarkable among ashes by its fine foliage, being much airier and lighter-textured than its kin. In winter, however, it is just another ash.

The Green Lake example is in the northeast section, south and slightly west of Corliss Avenue, near to the main asphalt path. May it prosper.

Quaking ASPEN
Populus tremuloides

GREEN LAKE'S two aspens are so small and young that their inclusion in this book is an act of hope; they are not so much trees as potential trees. The tallest, before commencing growth in 1992, is all of four feet. If you look closely, however, you can find the pair, growing very near the waterside on the narrow western strip of the lakeshore, about opposite the house on the southwest corner of Aurora and 70th Street.

Aspens have a vast native range in North America, being found on more acres than any other tree. The few Seattle native specimens were sacrificed at the altar of Urban Growth. Of thousands of aspens *planted* in the city, few show to supreme advantage their famous gold fall color, although they do produce slender, smooth, pleasingly pale trunks. There is, alas, no reason to expect the Green Lake youngsters to thrive: they need a less soggy site to color perfectly. They may, nevertheless, still gently flutter their distinctive roundish leaves in their matchless manner, making lakeside music.

European BEECH
Fagus sylvatica

WORDS of praise flow like water when it comes to the beech. All praise is due it. This symmetric tree has a nobly proportioned, smooth-barked, silvery-gray trunk serving as its eyecatching trademark. People love admiring beech trunks, touching them, speaking of them in elephantine words. Carving love hearts, too, happens, but cannot well be condoned. Far be it from me to discourage marks of affection, but a better celebration of commitment than initials in a trunk, is to *plant a tree*.

Beech is a giant shade tree, that happens also to bear little nuts in prickly husks. Since most of the nuts are hollow duds, and squirrels get nearly all of the few good ones, beechnuts are not a familiar dietary item to people—they taste vaguely like hazelnuts.

Green Lake has nine beeches on a woodsy knoll east of the ballfields. Most are crowding one another, and are therefore slender. One stands more unto itself, with a stout short trunk that divides into several sections.

Downy BIRCH
Betula pubescens

LIKE a poor cousin of everyone's favorite, the much planted European white birch, this tree is a weak version of North America's paper birch. Even in winter Downy Birch is easily distinguished because its dull gray twigs, held to the sky, reveal a dense *coating of short hairs*. Thus the name "pubescens." Most birch species have hair-free twigs. The ecologic role played by the hairs is unknown, but hairy leaves and plant parts usually have some reason for being. The ecologic role of the tree itself is as a fast-growing, usually short-lived, pioneer species.

Whatever its place in Europe's ecology, Downy Birch has always been shunned by nurseries and landscape designers, so is little known in cultivation. Its bark can be pleasingly whitish, but because the branching pattern of the tree is less graceful than that of the European white birch, it is comparatively rarely planted. In a word, it is a *coarser* tree. No longer offered at nurseries, enough *were* available long ago that Downy Birches are still easily located in Seattle, even wild ones now. Green Lake has 23, the most notable being a grove of 16 (with two European white birches) by the northwest parking lot.

At least one hybrid of Downy and European white birch is also present. Between the aforementioned grove of 16 and the Bathhouse Theatre, there are four birches: two are ordinary Whites, one is Downy, and one is a cross of the two species. Such hybrid birches share intermediate twig hairiness and other features. They were named *Betula × aurata* by Moritz Borkhausen (1760–1806). His Latin name means "gold-plated" birch. Since the White birch is also called Silver birch, and the Downy Birch bark is frequently pinkish-gold, maybe it was a bark color variation that sparked Borkhausen to nominally distinguish the hybrids in the first place? For my part, I freely admit that if the Downy Birch twigs were not *hairy*, I would have thought the trees were just variations of the commonly grown species. One can learn more and more about nature, but sometimes the distinctions seem less and less significant.

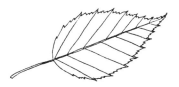

Paper BIRCH
Betula papyrifera

ALSO called Canoe Birch, this tree of Canada and the northern U.S. is world famous for having its distinctive hide made into canoes and other everyday utilities. Articles so constructed combine beauty, durability and watertightness. At Green Lake, like Seattle in general, the Paper Birch is nowhere near as common as its European cousin, the common white birch. The native's trunk is stouter, smoother, and wrapped like a mummy in irresistible white or copper-stained, peely bark. The leaves are much larger, borne on branches that lack the elegant dainty habit of the European. Oddly enough, the European grows wild all around the lake, but every Paper Birch was planted. The largest of 11 is west of the wading pool, its robust trunk 8¼ feet around.

White BIRCH
Betula pendula

OUTNUMBERING the other birches, this tree also outpolls them in humanity's popularity contest. Why? Other birches can also have snow white bark, but this is usually a comparatively airy and *slender* tree, that readily yields its pendulous tresses to the influence of the wind, thereby shimmering in lively beauty. Moreover, glowing gold in autumn glory as bright as the paper birch, it distinguishes itself from most European trees which have poorer fall color than their New World counterparts.

Green Lake has over 75 European White Birches, both planted and wild. Give it light, and it grows, be the soil ever so poor and wet; shade alone is its nemesis.

Weeping White Birch (*B. pendula* 'Tristis') is an even weepier, finer-textured selection. Weeping twigs on an otherwise regular tree characterize this variety. There are two other weeping birches: one with dissected or fern-cut leaves, the other a dwarf named 'Youngii' that drips densely as a mop. Neither of these varieties is at the park. Green Lake has about half a dozen 'Tristis' on the southeast shore, between the asphalt path and the water. Numerous typical European White Birches keep them company, but do not weep so obviously.

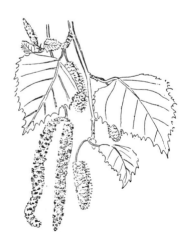

Yellow or Sweet BUCKEYE
Æsculus flava or *octandra*

THE "or" in my heading doesn't indicate doubt, but rather choice—this is *one* tree, yet known by a variety of names. Originally the tree was called "buckeye" because its ripe nuts, peeking through their split husks, reminded people of deer eyes. And it was called Sweet buckeye since it didn't stink like the Ohio buckeye. Yellow buckeye refers to its flower color, because most buckeye flowers are white, red or pink.

This species is native in the eastern and midwestern U.S., where it grows to be a stately, valuable forest tree. It is closely related to the horse-chestnut of Europe, but differs in three major ways: 1) it produces ho-hum floral ornament, mere homely yellow blossoms in May instead of the showstopping white horse-chestnut flowers of late April and early May; 2) it has spectacular fall color, not the usually unremarkable yellow brown of horse-chestnut; 3) it has much smoother bark and utterly smooth (not prickly) nut husks. In both species the nuts are poisonous raw. For the Horse-chestnut account see page 99.

Green Lake's only Yellow Buckeye grows northeast of the Pitch n' Putt golf course, its branches touching those of the park's lone red horse-chestnut, a smaller, much darker tree. In September it is richly and riotously colored, while its neighboring *Æsculus* is murky green. Its hollow trunk is not unusual; the wood has little rot-resistance and many of Seattle's old specimens are in similar imperfect shape.

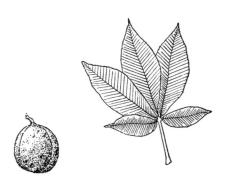

Northern CATALPA
Catalpa speciosa

IMPATIENT people sometimes condemn catalpas, because the trees are so slow to pop their buds and commence growing in spring. But consider the tree's point of view: it spends an extraordinary amount of energy when it finally does shoot forth, making gigantic leaves, flowers, and seedpods. Its leaves measure at least the size of these pages, some are twice as big; they are broadly rounded at their base, and terminate with a tip point. Losing their soft green, they fade to yellow in autumn. But catalpa is not grown solely for its bold foliage. During June the tree opens its big white flowers. *Then* it is a visual feast! No other Green Lake tree flowers approach the size of those of Northern Catalpa. Following the blossoms, fascinating "pencil pods" or "cigars" or "Indian beans" measuring 8–23 inches long are produced, and remain, green and dangling, for the rest of the summer and fall, before darkening, drying and dropping in winter. Each pod is stuffed full of small winged seeds.

From the eastern U.S., this species is also called the Hardy or Western Catalpa. It grows larger, produces longer pods, and has earlier, bigger blossoms than the Southern catalpa (treated on the next page).

Green Lake has one Northern Catalpa, with two smaller Southern catalpas, at the southeast part of the lake, northwest of the ballfields and Sunnyside Avenue.

Southern CATALPA
Catalpa bignonioides

"CATALPA" is derived from a North American Indian name. Two species grow in the U.S.; the rest are Asian or native in the West Indies. Big leaves, showy summer flowers, and most of all, slender seedpods, characterize the catalpas. Green Lake has a very odd Southern Catalpa north of the southwest parking lot. On this tree an upright sucker shoot must once have been broken somehow and left hanging to the ground. But it refused to wither and die; it healed and became, in effect, a *root*. You must see it to believe it.

Northwest of the ballfield area, by a bench overlooking the lake, are two Southern Catalpas with one larger Northern catalpa. Tell the two species apart even in winter by their bark and form: Northern catalpa trunks are straighter, more rugged, dark and furrowed; Southern Catalpa has comparatively thin, flaky bark on a frequently crooked or leaning trunk. Southern Catalpa flowers later, in July, and its popcorn-like flowers, its pods, and leaves, are all smaller.

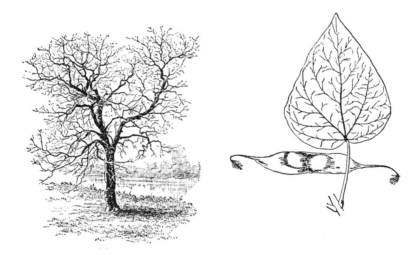

Atlas CEDAR
Cedrus atlantica

HYBRIDS and varieties excluded, Green Lake has 117 different tree species, and this is its lone African, hailing from the snow-clad Atlas Mountains of Algeria and Morocco. It's closely related to cedar of Lebanon, and to a lesser degree the deodar cedar. All three differ from other trees called cedars in that they bear *needles*, not scalelike miniature leaves. Atlas Cedar needles tend to be short and relatively blunt. Moreover, most Atlas Cedars seen are the silver-tinted or powder bluish *Cedrus atlantica* f. *glauca*. The light color of these is an uplifting, welcome contrast to the relentless dark green of most firs and other evergreens, that can be so depressing in our cloudy climate. The cones of Atlas Cedar are smaller than the fist-sized ones of the deodar and Lebanon cedars. As with those trees, the cones *shatter* and fall to the ground in pieces when the seeds ripen. Male trees, of course, produce only pollen, which is released in autumn.

Twenty Atlas Cedars are at Green Lake. Some are bluish enough to be designated *C. atlantica* f. *glauca*. A weirdly spidery one is on the skinny western strip of the lakeshore, south of 66th Street. The biggest Atlas Cedar, its trunk measuring a majestic 11 feet around, is near the Latona Avenue drive to the east parking-lot. It has lost some huge limbs in storms. Not far away to the southeast is one of the best baby-blue kinds, enveloping a Lawson Cypress.

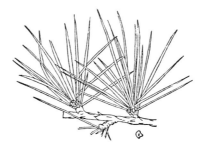

51

Deodar CEDAR
Cedrus Deodara

THE Sanskrit name of this renowned Himalayan tree translates "Tree of the Gods." Fortunately for us, Deodar is also very much a tree of the people, whether viewed as an object of beauty or as a commodious woodproducer in a forest of India. It's been in high favor since it was introduced to cultivation in the U.S. 150 years ago. A notice in the January 1852 *Horticulturist* periodical remarked how this tree was "the most popular of all the new evergreens yet proved in this country. It deserves its popularity. . . . Everybody is planting Deodars, and all the nurserymen are busy, importing and propagating them. Every large nursery in the country now advertises it, and the Deodar or Sacred Cedar of India, will in a few years we hope, be found in every ornamental plantation in the country."

Well, 140 years later Seattleites are indeed surrounded by goodlooking Deodars, since the tree performs better on the West Coast than anywhere else on the continent. But it doesn't thrive in the East. I will not try to describe the tree's special combination of inspiring size and delicate freshness—you will do better to go to the tree in living color and full life than rely on the black and white intimation offered here.

Green Lake has 17, and if you can only spare time for one, pay homage to the best of 3 specimens across the lawn east of the children's play area. Another exceptionally good example is at the north tip of the park by the intersection of Ashworth Avenue and 77th Street.

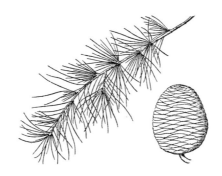

Incense CEDAR
Calocedrus decurrens

ALL cedars are fragrant. It is one of their basic attributes; for one to be unscented would be as odd as a square ball. But this native of Oregon and California has been singled out with the evocative, alluring name *Incense Cedar*. Why? John Muir, the illustrious mountaineer, exclaimed: "no waving fern-frond in shady dell is more unreservedly beautiful in form and texture, or half so inspiring in color and spicy fragrance." I must beg to differ. To me Incense Cedar is not markedly spicy in its fragrance: it smells exactly like pencil sharpener shavings. The amazing tangerine smell of Grand Fir, the potent, piercing juniper odor that can persist on human skin for hours, the fruity resinous richness of our own western red cedar—are all able to turn noses far more readily than can Incense Cedar. Nonetheless, what Incense Cedar *does* have, as Muir said, is a warm, rich *bright green color* that is especially heartwarming when contrasted with its equally striking cinnamon-red bark. So, in color and in its sentry-like shape the tree is most notable. It is definitely among the best ornamental conifers for planting in our area.

Green Lake has 28 on the southwest and south sides, mixed with Douglas firs north of the parking lot, and beyond the northeast part of the Pitch n' Putt golf course, too. Eye them, smell them, and enjoy them.

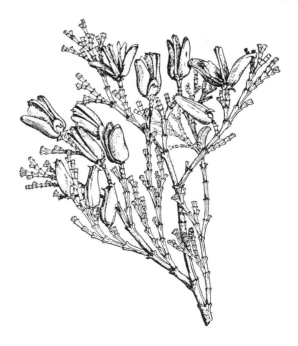

CEDAR of Lebanon
Cedrus libani

WASHINGTON'S tallest Cedar of Lebanon reigns at Green Lake. Towering 96 feet, it forms part of a dark evergreen tree screen by the northwest tennis courts, rubbing elbows as it were, with five of its kin as well as five eastern white pines and one Norway maple.

Cedar of Lebanon is the biblical cedar, famed for centuries. People have literally spent fortunes and risked life for this species. The fanfare over it originated in the time of King Solomon's temple, when, we learn (from the Bible and writings of the Jewish historian Josephus) that thousands of "hewers of wood" were drafted to "cut down many and large trees of cedar and cypress wood." For, in the Solomon's time, almost 3,000 years ago, the Cedar of Lebanon was just another commodity. Nowadays we consider it holy because of its role in history.

Great, in fact, is its height, broad its limbs, and year after year it grows more impressively huge. Even, then, without the associations it calls to our minds, it serves as a first-rate tree. Become acquainted with it by all means. More than a few Atlas cedars look so much like the classic ideal or stereotype of the Lebanese tree, that even tree experts confuse them every day of the week—so please, do not feel dumb if you have some doubts. Atlas cedars, besides being many times more abundant, are less dense in silhouette, with bluer, shorter, blunter needles, smaller and more numerous cones, lighter-colored bark, and have hairier twigs.

Curiously, the Green Lake specimens owe their planting to an irate lawyer. John P. Lycette lived across the street from the newly constructed west tennis courts in 1934, and complained in a detailed letter to the Park Department how the courts stood "stark and barren. . . in a rough, uncultivated area. . . quite unsightly." So to placate him, six cedars raised in the Park Department's nursery at Washington Park were promptly planted at Green Lake.

Western Red CEDAR
Thuja plicata

IT is *this* tree, rather than the hemlock, that should have been proclaimed Washington's State Tree. Pacific Northwest native Americans used and honored this cedar above all other trees. Its rot-defiant wood has been, is, and shall be in much greater demand than hemlock's run-of-the-mill wood. And the way cedar resists wind, enduring attacks of insects, ravages of fire and other travail for so long before dying, is inspiring. Yes, our hemlock is a worthy tree, truly king of its clan, well beloved, and not to be disparaged—but the red cedar is *still greater*, and so earns my vote. Incidentally, it is the trio of Douglas fir, western hemlock and western red cedar that dominate the evergreen forestland west of the Cascades; all people who live here should know these three trees.

Green Lake, in its pre-logging days, was ringed with mighty and old cedars, as well as alders and firs. Today there are only four planted ones, which still require some century or so of growth to command our attention to the utmost. Alas, one of the four, a two-trunked specimen surrounded by concrete north of the fieldhouse, looks to be not long for this world. However, an excellent pair are on Elm Hill (southwest of the Bathhouse Theatre) with five Norway spruces and three Norway maples. Another Western Red Cedar forms a grove with six Sawara cypresses north of the park's east side tennis courts. Perhaps, as straight streets and houses have replaced the mossy forest of early Seattle, it is appropriate that the natural or wild type of the cedar is outnumbered at Green Lake by its golden clone 'Zebrina' (next page).

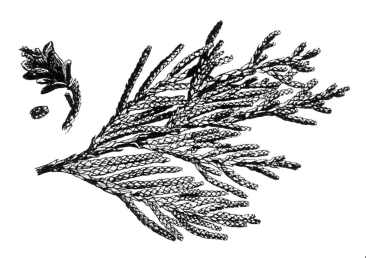

Zebra CEDAR
Thuja plicata 'Zebrina'

YELLOWISH-GOLD bands alternating with normal green, serve to mark this variety's foliage. The result is a cheerfully bright conifer, that differs from our customary seedling cedars not only in its color, but in being more of a huge shrub than a towering tree. Also, it makes fewer cones. Smell the crushed foliage, handle it, look at the bark—obviously it is a *variegated* sport of our native cedar. It arose in England probably, about 100 years ago, and is reproduced by cuttings or grafts. Thirty-one grow around Green Lake.

Bitter CHERRY
Prunus emarginata

SIXTEEN kinds of cherry trees grow at Green Lake. This species alone is native, and at that, has only a tenuous grip, being represented by merely one specimen. Every other cherry tree has prettier flowers, and most make better fruit and wood, too. Bitter Cherry's skinny twigs have small, drab leaves that might serve excellently as a textbook example of "plain." Its flowers are tiny and scarcely noticed. Its twigs stink if scratched—scratch and sniff should you care to be revolted. Its pea-sized fruit, translucent red, juicy, and austere at best, is more often repulsive. If all this is not bad enough, no Seattle native tree is sooner blown over by wind; don't look at it the wrong way—it might fall on you. Bitter Cherry grows with astonishing rapidity in sunny clearings, making groves of remarkably slender, shiny trunks. The *woodland beauty* of such trees, when they've achieved their ultimate size but not yet toppled, is more than sufficient to make up for their lack of strength or utility.

Green Lake's lone Bitter Cherry, at the north edge of a grove of mixed trees underplanted with *Forsythia* shrubs, between the fieldhouse and Ravenna Boulevard, is, sorry to say, nothing to write home about. It is approaching 40 feet tall, and its lowest twigs are nearly out of reach.

Higan CHERRY
Prunus subhirtella

TWENTY-FOUR Higan Cherries enliven the March landscape of Green Lake with pale pink flowers. They are finer textured and less flamboyant than most Japanese flowering cherries, and as a result have been cultivated less frequently. People prefer the passionate enthusiasm of bloom such as 'Kwanzan' Cherry offers, to the mellow restraint of ordinary Higan. For all that, Higans, bloom *earlier* than most of the showier sorts, extend the floral season, and give us an early joy, just before the explosive exuberance of the yoshino cherry—which somewhat resembles the Higan, though it's larger in every way, including visual impact. More likely than not, yoshino cherry is a Higan hybrid, perhaps the other parent being oshima cherry.

One Higan is on the lake's narrow southeastern shoreline (between Kirkwood Place and 63rd Street); the rest beautify the north side of the park, from northeast of the east tennis courts, to near 76th Street in the northwest section of the park.

Horinji CHERRY
Prunus 'Horinji'

RED-EYED flowers mark 'Horinji'. Each soft pink blossom's 12–15 petals fade almost to white, but the center remains reddish. The delicate flowers are easily shattered by wind or rain, and the tree is not of the strongest constitution, so comparatively few 'Horinji' are encountered. Green Lake has only one left: the southernmost cherry in the big bed of cherries and goldenchains west of the Bathhouse Theatre. The tree's short stout trunk divides into three sections, leaning toward a path to the parking lot. The name 'Horinji' refers to an ancient temple in Kyoto.

To the north, opposite 76th Street, keeping company with two larches, an Oriental spruce and a larger yoshino cherry is a **'Tanko-shinju'** cherry. It is extremely rare and can be mistaken for a 'Horinji'.

Kwanzan CHERRY
Prunus 'Kwanzan' (a.k.a. 'Sekiyama')

LIKE a sports hero or movie star, Kwanzan Cherry is outstanding, beloved, well known, and much publicized. Even so, like a batter not content to *hit* the baseball, but wanting to grandslam it, or a basketball player who insists on dunking, Kwanzan makes people gape in admiration of its hot pink blossoms borne in lavish profusion like masses of electrified cotton candy, before falling in a carpet of light pink snow. Forceful color goes hand in hand with a straightforward branch architecture: the tree is built like a soldier at attention—and, as with soldiers, doesn't grow soft and floppy until around age 45.

Green Lake is ringed by 95 Kwanzan Cherries. They bloom in April, and their young unfolding leaves are also flashy, being a rich reddish color before yielding to deep green. The blossoms consist of as many as 40 petals, so fruit is almost never set; the trees are grown by cuttings or are grafted on mazzard cherry rootstocks.

Mazzard CHERRY
Prunus avium

BIRDS are responsible for most of Green Lake's Mazzard Cherries. The rest no doubt came up as renegade rootstocks; none were intentionally planted. For this species of European wild cherry, also known as the Gean, is both happy as can be with Seattle's climate and soils, and bounteous in producing a cherry eagerly devoured by birds. Moreover, humans graft ornamental as well as fruiting cherries onto Mazzard rootstocks, and all too often the latter overwhelm and replace the intended scions. Therefore, Mazzards are common as wild trees in the Pacific Northwest. They are immensely stronger, larger and longer lived than our native bitter cherry, or than any other cherry trees we grow except the black cherry (*Prunus serotina*; not found at Green Lake).

Mazzard blooms in April and its flowers are dazzling white, quite like those of Sweet Cherry trees—which are simply improved derivatives of it. The fruit, ripe in June, is variously colored red, purple or even inky black, and can be scrumptious, or acid to an uncomfortable degree. The fall color is usually yellow but occasionally a rainbow of orange-red with green and yellow backdrops.

I counted 16 Mazzards at Green Lake, but could easily have overlooked some smaller ones. After all, the tree can be rather inconspicuous in December, coming up as it does wherever a bird chanced to drop a pit. Frankly, some of Green Lake's Mazzards should be cut down, for the benefit of the intentionally planted trees which they crowd out. A few which are easy to locate, are: one with the dying western red cedar north of the fieldhouse; six north of the Pitch n' Putt golf course.

Mikuruma-gaeshi CHERRY

Prunus 'Mikuruma-gaeshi'

A lovely name, 'Mikuruma-gaeshi' is said to have be given to a tree whose exquisite beauty so impressed the Japanese emperor, that the Royal Carriage *returned* from its course so the tree could be viewed again, and its delights savored at fitting leisure.

This variety is astonishingly rare: see it while you can. One is at Green Lake, another at Volunteer Park—no others are known in Seattle! The Green Lake tree is in the bed of cherries west of the Bathhouse Theatre. At the south end of the bed, it is evenly centered between the naden cherry, the horinji cherry, and an oshima cherry. Mikuruma-gaeshi flowers are pink with few extra petals, and bloom earlier than most associated cherry varieties; the tree grows distinctly wide rather than upright.

Naden CHERRY

Prunus × *Sieboldii*

ONCE I detested this tree, then merely disliked it, and if the trend continues, shall come to like it on occasion. Green Lake has only one Naden for you to judge by, so give it the benefit of the doubt. The tree is easily recognized, since unlike the other flowering cherries, its leaves are persistently, obviously *hairy* on both sides. The reason it sits low in my esteem is its gawky, constipated look. The flowers are a pretty pink color, but jammed in unseemly tight clusters, on an ingrown, crude twiggy crown, of poor vigor. Nonetheless, when beheld in full bloom on a sunny April day, only a scrooge or a snob can truthfully scoff at it. Another name for the Naden is Takasago, which means "Good health and long life!"

The Green Lake Naden is in the bed of cherries west of the Bathhouse Theatre. It is small, and leans markedly towards the theatre. It is practically on top of a *Philadelphus* or mock orange shrub. It is worth mentioning that at Leschi Park on Lake Washington there are three goodly Naden Cherries in the southeast corner, with locusts, poplars and a downy hawthorn.

Ojochin CHERRY
Prunus 'Ojochin'

LARGE blossoms characterize Ojochin. Pull out your ruler—the white or barely pink-blushed flowers can measure 2¼" inches wide! Appropriately, its Japanese name means "large lantern." Few extra petals beyond the obligatory five are borne, but with those produced being so huge, who needs more? Ojochin is unfortunately rare, with only one at the park, about in the middle of the Bathhouse Theatre cherry bed, on the west side, out in the open, growing toward the southwest because that is where the sunshine is. Even when the tree is not displaying its lovable, big flowers, its broad, often bluntish leaves are distinctive.

Oshima CHERRY
Prunus Lannesiana var. *speciosa*

THREE Oshima Cherries are in the Bathhouse Theatre cherry bed. Two resemble one another and are probably Oshima *hybrids*, but the third is true as can be. This species is rarer in local cultivation than the other Japanese cherries, but is every bit as nice. The flowers are big and smell sweet, borne on long-stalked clusters in late March and early April. They are white or faintly pink. Few if any extra petals are present. A number of Seattle specimens I've called Oshima Cherries are in all likelihood some nameable hybrid clones. The problem is, no one in this country is sufficiently familiar with these Japanese trees to attach proper names confidently to the varieties present in our parks. This neglect upsets me, so I am gradually acquiring the needed familiarity and will endeavor to share what I learn with everyone who wants to know.

The largest tree of all in the Bathhouse bed is an Oshima with white flowers. Two smaller Oshimas, differing from the big one in having pink flowers, are also present—one just *north* of the big one in a crowded situation; the other far to the *southwest* of the bed, with a horinji and a mikuruma-gaeshi cherry trees. The Oshima is the closest of these three cherries to the three adjacent multitrunked goldenchains.

Shiro-fugen CHERRY
Prunus 'Shiro-fugen'

COMPARED to its siblings, this popular cherry might be called a nonconformist, or an exhibitionist! Certainly a *character*. Shiro-fugen raises eyebrows by having flowers that come from tight pink buds, opening to white, then fading pinkish, and some of them amazingly endure into June or July, even August in some years! The flowers dangle notably, and have 20 to 32 petals, in the midst of which are conspicuous leafy green affairs (transfigured reproductive organs, no less). Its name means "white goddess" or "white red" and refers to the powerful, dramatic contrast between the pale flowers and very dark reddish young expanding leaves. The tree is less coarse than bully kwanzan, with relatively slender twigs and less heavy effusiveness of bloom. Green Lake has seven on the northeast side, from Orin Court to Ravenna Boulevard.

Shirotae or Mt. Fuji CHERRY
Prunus 'Shirotae' or 'Mt. Fuji'

NEXT to kwanzan this is the most popular of all the big, fluffy Japanese flowering cherries known collectively as the Sato Zakura. It grows wide, as if being invisibly squashed from above. Its flowers are immaculate white, and its young leaves absolutely green. The purity thus exemplified serves as a wonderful contrast to the other heavily pigmented flowering cherries. Another desirable quality of Shirotae is its earliness of bloom: in March. The flowers are fairly big, with 5–8 (11) petals, and are faintly fragrant.

Green Lake has just two old ones: a pair near a ukon cherry (told by its yellowish flowers), northwest of the Bathhouse Theatre. Also, the four corners of the fieldhouse-Evans Pool building have youngsters.

Sour CHERRY *hybrid*
Prunus × *Gondouinii* 'Schnee'

SOUR Cherries, also called Pie or Tart Cherries, are tres normally seen only in orchards or back yards. The gleaming fruit is a familiar sight, and differs from sweet cherries not only in taste, but in often hanging very long on the tree, even into September. Sour Cherry is a twiggy small tree with *dark* green foliage, sparsely borne. The growth rate is moderate, but the tree stays small, putting its energy into luscious big cherries. It can be distinguished from sweet cherry by its small size, skinny drooping branches, and small, relatively *rounded* dark green, hairless and shiny leaves, which have late, dull fall color before dropping. Little ball-like clusters of pure white flowers in April appear on the naked twigs. The cherries are variously colored but usually *bright* red and very showy, not to mention delicious.

Green Lake's lone example is, however, an *ornamental hybrid* instead of a fruit-producing variety. "Schnee" is the German word for snow. The Snow or Schnee Cherry is a fruitless Duke or Royal Cherry, as sweet cherry / sour cherry hybrids are called. Although sterile, Snow Cherry is pretty in bloom and useful for its exceptional cold hardiness and compact growth form. Wilhelm Pfitzer of Stuttgart originated it about 1920. Until 1959 it was scarcely planted in the U.S. Then it was widely advertised by Scanlon nurseries of Ohio as *Prunus avium* 'Scanlon' or *Prunus avium* 'Globe'.

Green Lake's single Snow Cherry is at the northwest part of the park, south of Elm Hill, next to the unpaved trail that goes from the parking lot to the huge granite boulder near the asphalt lakeside path. Between the Snow Cherry and golden rain tree grove is a kwanzan cherry. The Snow Cherry trunk forks at about six feet into three sections.

Temari CHERRY
Prunus 'Temari'

TENNIS ball sized clusters of dense, frilly flowers, colored white with a whisper of pink, decorate the knobby bare branches of Temari in April. The flower petals are attractively fringed with tiny teeth. When the leaves finally appear, rather belatedly, they, too, are bristly-edged. Compared to kwanzan and similar pompom-weight flowering cherries, the *tightly-packed* flowerbuds give away Temari's identity even in winter. Its floral color is endearing and distinctive, too: not white, not rosy pink, but somewhere in between. Temari is not rare in Seattle, but has not been planted in recent years. It is no longer in the North American nursery trade.

Green Lake has one north of a row of seven kwanzan (and a ukon) cherries bordering the northwest parking lot; and two by the intersection of 71st and Ravenna Boulevard. There, the one Temari is rather in the shadow of a sycamore maple. The other, to its south beyond a grove, is leaning; its trunk is small and rotting.

Ukon CHERRY
Prunus 'Ukon'

YELLOWISH flowers are this cherry's claim to a unique place in the ranks of cherries. Do not expect a spectacular lemon yellow, though—Ukon gives instead a gentle pale yellow-green, with even a tiny bit of pink mixed in sometimes. When not blooming, it looks the world like kwanzan cherry and might thus be considered, as far as tree form and foliage are considered, as a yellow-flowered kwanzan. But in spring, when color is the center of people's attention, Ukon reveals itself as very different. Its flowers are lighter in weight as well as being yellowish. There are only 5–12 petals. The young unfolding leaves are olive green or slightly bronzy.

Green Lake has 14 in the north part, from the northwest parking lot to Ravenna Boulevard.

Whitcomb CHERRY
Prunus subhirtella 'Whitcombii'

BRIGHT, *strong pink* blossoms refreshingly early in spring, and a vigorous, broad branching pattern, distinguish this higan cherry variety. Like all higan varieties, it has thin, hairy twigs, and small, profuse flowers with narrow petals. Interestingly, it is a local find: the original specimen came from the estate of David Whitcomb, of Woodway Park near Richmond Beach, over 50 years ago. Now the tree is abundant, and sold at numerous nurseries.

Green Lake has only one Whitcomb Cherry, rather young, north of the fieldhouse, in a bed of St. John's-wort groundcover west of the trash dumpster (a yoshino cherry is east of the dumpster). February-March sees Whitcomb Cherry in flower.

Yoshino CHERRY
Prunus × *yedoensis*

IN Yoshino Cherry, a chance hybrid, nature has combined the excellent triad of perfect beauty, constitutional strength, and a scale that is large and copious but neither coarse nor gaunt. It may be *the best* flowering cherry tree for these reasons. So many other varieties are weak, or like bimbos, are good-looking only when in bloom—heavy dull things otherwise. Not Yoshino. Yoshino blooms during late March and early April, after most of the higan cherries (which have smaller, pinker flowers) but before the double-flowered fullness of the kwanzan clan (Sato Zakura), making Green Lake (with 41 of them) white with fleecy petals.

The largest cherry trees in the park are Yoshino, excepting some taller, slender mazzards. In June some small black cherries ripen. Yoshino comes largely "true" from seed, although most are grown by cuttings or grafts. The largest Yoshino in the park is on the northeast strip of the lakeshore, not far from Sunnyside Avenue, its trunk over 7½ feet around.

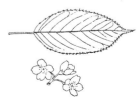

Black COTTONWOOD
Populus trichocarpa

COTTONWOODS are monstrous giants. They are Green Lake's largest trees. The park's north part, especially, has landmark specimens of these great trees dominating the scenery. They are easily the tallest trees, seen from afar. The grove of 28 at Gaines Point is an often-photographed spot. The largest trunks are straight gray pillars 10 to 12 feet in circumference.

Nature's price for bestowing such vast size in a short time, however, is an abbreviated lifespan. Every year cottonwoods at Green Lake drop limbs or collapse altogether. Conks, the reproductive bodies of wood-decaying fungi, live on some of their trunks; the roots are frequently seen raised above the grass and damaged by mowers, revealing rot within. During June, female trees release the whitish downy seeds that give the species its popular name. In November and early December the leaves, formerly dark lustrous green on top and whitish beneath, turn to gold and fall to the earth.

Bald CYPRESS
Taxodium distichum

GREEN LAKE'S 102 Bald Cypresses are a magnificent presence, vivid in color, fine in texture and grand in their landscape scale. No other West Coast planting of this southern U.S. species is so extensive or noteworthy. Bald Cypress is a member of the redwood family, and grows to immense size in its swampy homeland. Besides being big, it stands out in the way its delicate green frond-like leaflets turn rusty colored, then red or purplish-brown, before eventually dropping in late fall. Every winter this brings forth concerned questions about "the dying evergreens at Green Lake." Every spring the trees awaken from their dormancy and grow anew.

The trunks are vaguely like those of Seattle's native cedar, with reddish-brown, soft, fibrous bark. The cones are knobby, roundish or egg-shaped, 1-1½ inches long, and usually fall to pieces to release the seeds when ripe in winter. Such seeds were the favorite food of the long-extinct Carolina parakeet. "Cypress knees" are root-like conical projections peculiar to this species, and can be found as tall as 14 feet in nature. So far, Green Lake has only a few little beginnings bumping out of the ground—as the years go by more will appear, and people who trip over them will develop an especially keen awareness of their presence. The tallest Green Lake Bald Cypress is over 100 feet, and the stoutest trunk more than 8 feet around.

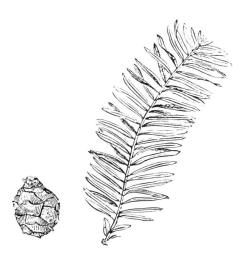

Hinoki CYPRESS
Chamæcyparis obtusa

ONLY two Hinoki Cypresses grow at Green Lake, and they are a small, unmemorable pair, by the asphalt path near the Aqua Theatre, right next to a considerably larger plumose sawara cypress, and two colorful young sorrel trees. Hinoki foliage is dark and arranged in softly rounded sprays of scales, intermittently mixed with round cones about the size of holly berries. "Hi-noki" means fire tree, and the cones at their stage of ripeness and seed-dispersal do have a sort of fiery red glow of much appeal. The winter of 1990–91 was excruciatingly hard for Hinoki Cypresses locally, but normally these Japanese evergreens are perfectly hardy, eminently choice ornamentals.

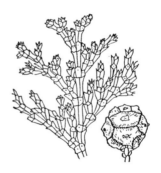

Lawson CYPRESS
Chamæcyparis Lawsoniana

EARTH'S most variable conifer, has, for better or worse, been planted with restraint at Green Lake. Therefore, instead of many cultivated varieties needing to be described and rendered distinctive from one another, the situation is simple. There are 58 ordinary Lawson Cypress seedlings (25 of them being near the children's play area), and a handful of varieties. It might have been far more complex. Lawson Cypress (foresters call it **Port Orford Cedar**) is an Oregon evergreen that has achieved notoriety by having a small natural range, but practically unlimited ability to modify its appearance in cultivation. Thus, there are green, blue, variegated, yellow, dense, diaphanous, dwarf, varieties of any shape and size: only the *odor* and *wood structure* seems to be constant.

However, a threatening rot-root disease (Phytophthora) is killing Lawson Cypresses left and right, so nurseries have drastically reduced propagating them. West of the Cascades always was the preferred region of these trees, and as long as specimens remain uninfected they shall continue to beautify and cleanse our planted landscape.

Surprisingly, Green Lake's population is not infected yet, or I have missed noticing any of the telltale browning and dying.

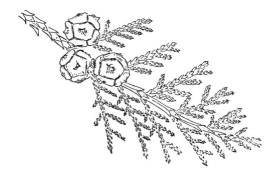

Blue Lawson CYPRESS

Chamæcyparis Lawsoniana f. *glauca*

WHEN Lawson Cypress trees raised from seed are comparatively bluish instead of pure green, they can be designated by this general name. The *best* of the blues have been in turn named and grafted—but none of the latter perfections grace Green Lake. However, two bluish seedlings happen to be in the vicinity of the children's play area (*i.e.*, northeast of the Evans Pool building), one of them being in a grove of a dozen Lawson Cypresses around the restrooms by 72nd Street, the other in a similar grove of seven trees near the sidewalk by the parking lot.

Scarab Lawson CYPRESS

Chamæcyparis Lawsoniana 'Allumii'

DUSKY bluish or steely-gray green foliage on a broad-based, upswept tree, characterize this conifer. Eight grow by the caretaker's building near 77th Street at the north tip of the lake. This odd form arose over one hundred years ago, and has been among the most popular and widely planted of all Lawson Cypresses.

Weeping Lawson CYPRESS

Chamæcyparis Lawsoniana 'Intertexta'

RIGHT by the children's play area northeast of the Evans Pool building, are two of the very rare, dark, slender specimens of this striking Lawson cypress, the taller measuring fifty feet. 'Intertexta' originated about 1869 at Lawson's Edinburgh nursery. Up close, you will find the weeping sprays of scaly foliage are thick, hard, and sparse. Although these trees are attractive, precious few exist in our area, and no larger ones are known. It can be propagated by rooting foot-long cuttings taken anytime from November to February.

Leyland CYPRESS
× *Cupressocyparis Leylandii*
(Cupressus macrocarpa × *Chamæcyparis nootkatensis)*

INSPIRATION can come as a creative flash in a moment, or can present itself as an attractive new option, which we embrace in hope it will work better than that which we abandon. Leyland Cypress, it seems, has been the nursery industry's answer to the dying Lawson cypresses. Both kinds are variable, easily propagated dense evergreens, excellent for planting as screens. But Leyland Cypress is much more rampant and tough, probably because it resulted as the hybrid offspring of the Monterey cypress of California fame, and the Alaska yellow cedar, a Pacific Northwest native.

In any case, Leyland Cypress grows mighty fast, is resistant to adversity, and attains large dimensions. Thanks to its variability, we do not *need* to keep planting the common hideously dark form; we can instead plant the light-colored Naylor's Blue and Castlewellan Gold selections. Green Lake, alas, has seven of the unrelenting dark green kinds planted recently against the fieldhouse/pool building. Small still, while these words are fresh, the seven will soon enough be big dark blobs, soaking up light, hulking out from the walls, daring people to try admiring them.

Sawara CYPRESS
Chamæcyparis pisifera

JAPAN has enriched our ornamental tree population in a tremendous way since the 1850s; rather few acquisitions preceded that period. The Sawara Cypress and its varieties, once called *Retinospora*, made a great hit after they were imported to this country by Dr. George Hall (1820–1899) in April, 1861. For many decades thereafter they were extensively planted wherever the climate allowed.

Sawara, like its close relative Lawson cypress, gave rise to rich diversity of colors and shapes. Green Lake has 35 wild version or "natural" Sawara Cypresses, and small quantities of various garden varieties (the latter are treated on the following two pages).

If you walk straight north of the park's east side tennis courts, you will come to a grove that consists of six Sawara Cypresses and one of our western red cedars. The lone native is the tallest, stoutest-trunked, and most fully foliated. You can see why, therefore, the Sawara Cypress in its wild form has been long unavailable at nurseries—people prefer lusher, denser evergreens.

Golden Sawara CYPRESS
Chamæcyparis pisifera 'Aurea'

GOLDEN-tinged new spring growth sets this apart from ordinary Sawara Cypresses. Maybe also this form is a tad smaller. By winter, however, the gold is faded to an almost imperceptible yellow-green. There is one of these trees on the northeast strip of the lakeshore between Orin and 77th Street; and two are on the north shore between 77th and 78th. In May and June they stand out somewhat. Otherwise they are nondescript, neither glittering nor golden.

Moss Sawara CYPRESS
Chamæcyparis pisifera f. *squarrosa*

HIGHLY distinctive and utterly unlike the regular Sawara, this is a permanent juvenile stage of foliage on a full-size tree. By "juvenile" is meant the sort of appearance characterizing most year-old cedar, cypress and juniper seedlings. That is, instead of green, scaly foliage and profuse production of tiny round cones, the Moss Sawara makes fluffy, soft gray masses of short, juniper-like needles.

This form has been planted by the millions, but not more than nine are at Green Lake. Three are east and northeast of the east tennis courts, *with* four plume Sawara Cypresses and fourteen regular Sawara Cypress for ease of comparison. Six are in another mixed Sawara grove, along with a zebra cedar, near where the path heading north from Sunnyside Avenue joins the lake's main perimeter path southwest of the ballfields.

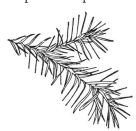

Plume Sawara CYPRESS
Chamæcyparis pisifera f. *plumosa*

IF the problem for regular Sawara Cypresses' lack of appeal is its plain, commonplace habit, Plume Sawara is the solution, because this version is luxuriously dense and billowy, at least while young and vigorous. In age, as with people, it thins and slows. The foliage fronds are, whether borne densely or not, *thick* and *crispy*, and either green or yellow-green, though Green Lake's 20 specimens are all quite appropriately greenish.

Thread Sawara CYPRESS
Chamæcyparis pisifera f. *filifera*

SKELETAL outlining of the foliage, caused by the main twigs lengthening at the expense of the secondary ones, makes the string or threadbranch Sawara an open, if not gaunt, semi-pendulous small tree. In the case of Green Lake's nine specimens, some only hint at this quality—evidently they are reverting to the usual foliage mode, thereby diluting their distinctiveness. All nine are on the northeast shore, from Bagley Avenue to beyond the caretaker's building by 77th Street. They are unattractive for the most part.

Cornelian Cherry DOGWOOD
Cornus mas

WARMTH is the gist of life. Some trees bring about a warm feeling in people from the way their beauty influences us, exactly as music thrills us, touching a respondent chord. Cornelian Cherry, a large shrub or small tree brightly blooming with a multitude of sparkling yellow flowers in winter, is such a sunshiny tree. Nothing like familiar dogwood flowers, nor like any cherry blossoms, they resemble in their yellow impact the winter-blooming witch hazel, winter jasmine and forsythia.

But Cornelian Cherry, unlike those shrubs, follows its February flowers with the fruit for which it was named. In August and onward, red fruit appears, ripening to deep maroon or ruby-rich, soft, juicy, edible cherries. Pick them only when they're ready to fall of their own accord at the slightest tug. Don't expect them to taste of cherries; let their own flavor gratify you.

Cornelian Cherry deserves our applause, then, for its cheerfully colorful flowers in winter, when we most need a lift, and for producing delectable fruit, as well as being a strong, troublefree tree. Its one imperfection is dismal fall leaf color.

Green Lake's population of these European trees consists of two youngsters planted in 1990 next to an eastern dogwood in a heart-shaped bed at the north end of the lake by the intersection of a major path from N 77th Street and the lakeshore path. Since the specimens planted were small, and will flower sparingly until they are much larger, it will be a few years before people start to take much notice of them. Yet when they do grow up and wear their winter halo of tiny gold flowers, all eyes will devour their unrivaled glory.

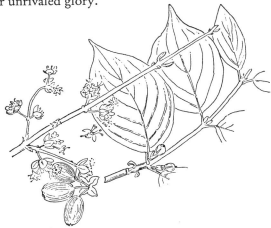

Eastern DOGWOOD
Cornus florida

EASTERN North Americans know this dogwood well: it's one of the commonest, most readily recognized flowering trees, displaying big white or pink blossoms in late April or early May. Following the flowers are little orange-red berries of shining beauty, but of flavor bitter beyond telling. The autumn leaf color, too, can be a superb red. Nor does the dogwood's winter aspect lack appeal, for the silvery twigs curved up at their ends and tipped by tiny flowerbud buttons form a handsome tracery. Even the checkered bark of older trunks is interesting. Altogether, few small trees are so ideal for human enjoyment. Varieties by the dozens have been raised and named. Only, recently disease has caused such severe damage that people have begun turning more towards kousa dogwood to replace this American native.

Green Lake's north side is planted with 18 older specimens. Unfortunately, these are average seedlings—mere shadows of the improved, grafted varieties featuring larger, more abundant flowers. Three younger Eastern Dogwoods are also present: one with the two cornelian-cherry dogwoods. A second youngster is opposite Stone Avenue in the long narrow bed of flowering cherries and golden rain trees flanking the northwest parking lot. The third is a pink-flowered, four-trunked one on the fieldhouse patio.

Kousa DOGWOOD
Cornus Kousa

POISED on the threshold of popularity, Kousa Dogwood is a Far Eastern tree of connoisseur quality. Although *perfect* trees are more the stuff of imagination than everyday sights, Kousa truly comes as close as any to the exalted title of an *ideal* small ornamental tree. Why? Its bark, in age at least, is attractively flaky and particolored. Its branching habit of a fan shape opening ever wider over the years, displays to excellent advantage its dazzling masses of starry flowers in June. Though white to begin with, the flowers frequently assume a pink tinge as they fade. Following are stalked red fruit resembling big, dull strawberries or raspberries, though gritty with seeds, and flavored a trifle oddly. Autumn color can be burgundy or red, and is usually choice.

Several years ago it was difficult to obtain more than a couple of Kousa Dogwood varieties. Now, over 30 cultivated varieties have been named, and some hybrids of the species with eastern dogwood also exist. Hence, many more Kousas are coming into our lives. Green Lake has 11 bushy, small, closely planted specimens near the Aqua Theatre, and two slender, water-thirsty ones north of the wading pool, in the shadow of birches.

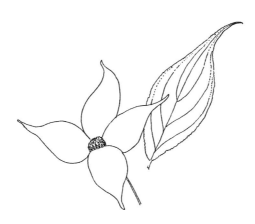

Pacific DOGWOOD
Cornus Nuttallii

PREMIER among Pacific Northwest native trees for floral effect, this West Coast dogwood tests our patience with its disease susceptibility. Seattle of yesteryear was far whiter in April, with many more splendid dogwoods in flower, than nowadays. This sad decline has been caused not so much by the tree's naturally brief lifespan and resentment of environmental disturbance, as by an introduced leaf fungus (*Discula*) known as anthracnose. As a result, those of us who love dogwoods are anguished: we see the trees sick, disfigured, as blemished with blight as they were formerly resplendent in beauty.

Just as radiant health is difficult to capture in words on paper, so is its antithesis. But when you view Green Lake's several native dogwoods, please understand that they cannot be blamed for their suffering, and we can do practically nothing to help them.

Two old wrecks are on the grassy slope southwest of the ballfields, beyond Sunnyside Avenue; they stand about 20 feet west of an English yew. A young couple are west of the Pitch n' Putt golf course, growing right next to a boulder—one on each side. Pacific Dogwoods usually produce a second crop of flowers in late summer and fall, so we have an additional opportunity to gaze at their beauty.

American White ELM
Ulmus americana

AN American Elm might well be planted on the doorstep of heaven. Anyone who thinks such a suggestion presumptuous or unseemly, must be excused as one who has not yet seen this noble species grown to perfection. White Elm is the tree exalted above all by some of the world's most ardent tree enthusiasts. Being in love with this tree is a great joy: the feeling *lasts* and is always uplifting, an infusion of positive energy. Since Seattle does not have the desolating Dutch Elm Disease, we who live in or visit this rare piece of earth, are able to indulge in elms to our heart's content.

In botany books you can read about the elm's veiny, lopsided leaves, edged by jagged teeth; its microscopic flowers and flimsy winged seeds, too, are given description. But the essence or soul of this elm is in its grand size and shape, not in transient details of color or wood qualities. If you can view the four American Elms at Green Lake, on the hill southwest of the Bathhouse Theatre, and not be moved to any reverence, not feel any sensory delight, then you may be immune to the subtle emanations or messages of any natural wonders.

Once on Elm Hill, it is easy to distinguish the one European smoothleaf elm from the four Americans: even in winter the branch structure is dissimilar—the Americans are like antelopes, the European like a bear. These elms were probably planted in 1932 to commemorate the 200th anniversary of the birth of George Washington (1732–1799). The landmark boulder by the path once held a plaque that might've told as much. A fifth American elm, torn and deformed by storms, stands hulking on the southeast shore, tilted away from the fieldhouse, west of where Sunnyside Avenue intersects the park.

Hybrid ELM
Ulmus × hollandica

SMOOTHLEAF Elm, treated on page 82, frequently hybridizes, and one of these hybrid elms is at Green Lake. This cross differs from purebred smoothleaf elms by having larger, rougher, hairier leaves, with more veins, on shorter stalks, of darker color and thicker texture. The seeds are bigger, too. In a word, the hybrid might be called comparatively masculine. All of these differences resulted from the influence of Wych Elm (*Ulmus glabra*, not at Green Lake), one of its parents.

Standing on the beach southwest of the fieldhouse, it is larger than the elm north of it, and more vigorous. The elm north of it is probably a smoothleaf elm, or may *also* be a hybrid, but is too far out of reach for proper identification.

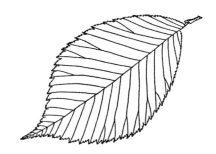

Siberian ELM
Ulmus pumila

CHINESE Elm is the general U.S. name for this species, but we who write tree books, for no good reason, stubbornly title it "Siberian" Elm. The species has a vast Asiatic range, and both names may be fairly challenged as to their appropriateness. In any case, the tree bears small leaves, usually less than two inches long. Or to put it another way they are almost never larger than the size of a teaspoon, which makes them *small* compared to most elm leaves. The leaves are medium green in color and are thin. Altogether they are decidedly plain. The winged seeds, produced in late spring, are conspicuously roundish, unlike most elm seeds, though they're just as flat. They're hairless, unlike American white elm seeds. The tree is twiggy with brittle gray branchlets, and it has no sublimity of form, though it can be ruggedly handsome and impressively large.

Green Lake has four on the narrow western lakeshore, south of 67th Street. A fifth is very small and slender, on the north side of the park, between the lake and wading pool, leaning toward the pool.

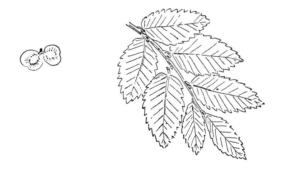

Smoothleaf ELM
Ulmus minor

THE main elm of Europe, north Africa and Asia Minor, a species noteworthy for its astonishing variation, travels under this name (sometimes it's styled *Ulmus carpinifolia*). The French call it "orme," Germans say "ulme," in Dutch it's "olm" or "iep," and the Spaniards call it "olmo." Although North America's half-dozen elm species are considered distinctive, well-known entities, the Old World elm population is complex and puzzling. Unlike American elms, most European elms readily reproduce by root suckers as well as by seeds. Because the trees were so useful to people, thousands of years of human cultivation resulted in blurring of original species' ranges, and much hybridization occurred. So now a baffling plethora of European elms exists, and their naming provides full-time work for specialists. What a job!

Smoothleaf Elms show no end of variability in *shape*, but they never achieve the peculiar transcendent grandeur of the American white elm. Their leaves are indeed often smooth, but can be rough as sandpaper, of relatively small to middling size, with few, widely spaced veins. The winged seeds are small and hairless, often teardrop-shaped.

Green Lake has one with the four American elms on Elm Hill southwest of the Bathhouse Theatre. It is the dense, low, broad tree, staying green much later in autumn than the others. A second Smoothleaf Elm (possibly a hybrid) grows north of the hybrid elm (which is larger than the Smoothleaf and has less checkered bark), on the beach southwest of the fieldhouse. This second Smoothleaf Elm differs from the Elm Hill specimen.

Common FIG
Ficus Carica

SOMEONE with spunk planted a fig tree on the northeast shore of Green Lake in early October, 1991. It is between Meridian and Orin, closer to the former, quite close to the memorial bench set in concrete and dedicated to Maury Hagen, Junior. Well, for optimal fruit production, a warm site would have been better. Heat ripens figs. The cold winds of north Green Lake will do no good for this Mediterranean native. Still, there is something fun about having a classic tree at the park for everyone to see. The twigs are stout; the leaves are correspondingly large, late to unfold in spring, curiously lobed, hairy, of a deep green color and thick texture. The fruit is well known, but whether any will *ripen* on the Green Lake specimen we shall see. The season will be late summer and fall. Don't get caught napping.

Caucasian FIR
Abies Nordmanniana

NUMEROUS non-native firs have been planted in our region, and this species from the Caucasus mountains is one of the most successful, handsome and common. It grows very tall, making a dark, narrow, densely foliated tree. Flat, blunt "needles" dark on top and pale underneath, are thickly arranged around the twigs, although mostly arrayed on the upper side. Contrasting pleasingly with the dark boughs, the bark is hard, smooth, and silvery gray. The cones, borne only near the top of the crown, are about the size and shape of cucumbers, and showy, but become dry and break to pieces in late summer, thereby liberating the seeds to the whims of the wind.

Green Lake's trees are probably too young to make cones. There are three Caucasian Firs with a Greek fir at the south part of the lake, east of the Aqua Theatre; and one (with a leaning green Colorado spruce) on the northeast strip of the lakeshore, not far from Sunnyside Avenue.

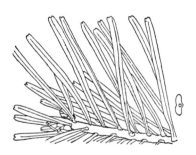

Douglas FIR
Pseudotsuga Menziesii

ABUNDANCE and importance go together when speaking of Douglas Firs at Green Lake. With 110 specimens present, it is the park's commonest tree; and in terms of both ecology and economics, this species is the Pacific Northwest's most important tree. Since Green Lake was shorn of its old-growth fir forest in pioneer days, it is only proper that saplings have been replanted for our children to inherit. People who are busy can afford to feel indifferent to most trees, but anyone who wants a basic or essential understanding of nature in the Northwest should know about Douglas Firs. What may seem superlative language is necessary to merely catalog the *facts* about this influential species. Although Green Lake has only comparatively young examples (the oldest are in the golf course), Seattle in general has plenty of older, larger ones; in some parks it is easy to find Douglas Firs *more than 200 feet tall.*

Greek FIR
Abies cephalonica

FREED from the ravaged soils of its old, weary land, and planted in rich earth receiving much rainfall, Greek Fir grows prodigiously. If anything, it tends to become too large for most places where we might want a tree. Unlike most fir species, the Greek is generally endowed with sharp needles, as in spruces, and moreover grows wide instead of the more common narrow mode. Few landscapes schemes in our cities, however, can accommodate broad, prickly, gargantuan evergreens.

Green Lake has only two, both perhaps somewhat over 30 years old. One is with three Caucasian firs east of the Aqua Theatre. The second is on the northeast lakeshore, a bit west of Bagley Avenue, opposite house #7556; it splits at just over six feet height into two trunks.

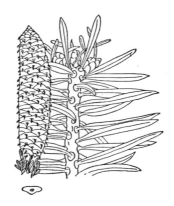

Veitch FIR
Abies Veitchii

JAPANESE Alpine Fir, or Japanese Silver Fir, are more descriptive names for this slender tree. Shirabiso or Shirabe are its Japanese names. The Veitch family was of supreme importance in British horticulture, so it is no surprise that numerous plants bear their name. Specifically, the tree name commemorates John Gould Veitch (1839–1870), who introduced this species to England in 1860.

Two characteristics distinguish Veitch Fir: its trunk is smooth, pale gray, and often looks like rippling muscles near the base; its needles are wide, blunt, and shimmering, vivid whitish on their undersides. In beauty of foliage it is as lovely, close-up, as any fir. But the tree can look scrawny unless perfect growing conditions prevail—ample sunshine, moisture at the root, and loose, organic soil. In an average, exposed Seattle site, subject to dry summer spells and wind, there is stress written on the tree's every part. It hasn't the strength to endure in general cultivation, so Seattle's population, which was much larger 50 years ago, has declined yearly.

Green Lake has 19 remaining. Every year it seems more of them die. One, as far as trunk size goes, is the largest specimen known in Washington. It grows with another Veitch, and a Douglas fir, on the park's narrow southeast strip, opposite Kirkwood Place. This record-size tree stands 50 feet tall, and its trunk measures 5'5" around. Most of the other Veitch Firs are at the northwest part of the park, near the tennis courts.

White FIR
Abies concolor

LONG, flattened, bluish needles prettily colored and laid out in a soft, lush, curvy, way that begs for caressing, make White Firs lovable so they are frequently planted. The species is a western U.S. native, with a strong ability to grow well in many soils and temperature ranges. Its ornamental role is directly equivalent to that of the blue Colorado spruce, which differs from the fir in bearing shorter, spiny needles, and in having rough, scratchy twigs and bark. White Fir also grows larger than the spruce, yet doesn't live as long in cultivation.

Green Lake's eleven specimens range from three youngsters planted in 1991 (which are greener than the older ones), to the largest of all, growing with three pin oaks and five evergreen magnolias in an island of grass and trees at the east parking lot.

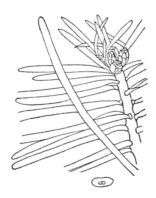

GINKGO
Ginkgo biloba

FOREMOST in books that arrange trees by evolutionary sequence, Ginkgo has the distinction of being earth's most ancient tree, a true living fossil. Like horsetails and tree ferns, this Chinese tree has endured through so many *millions of years* that we, mere transient specks of secondary life compared to these prehistoric plants, cannot comprehend the length of their existence: such reckoning is beyond human ability. People think they have accomplished something to trace their family tree back to the year 1500, but there are Ginkgos still alive that were born centuries before then. Belittling human achievement in order to celebrate the mute progression of arboreal life is not my intent. Simply, we must revere the Ginkgo as the ultimate survivor in the long run of geologically-measured evolution. For it has withstood floods, ice ages, volcanism, continental drift, and who knows what else, far longer than any other tree.

Ginkgo is easily recognized by its strange fan shaped leaf, split at the end, leading to the English name Maidenhair Tree. In addition to possessing unique shape, the leaves are unequalled for fall color, consistently turning as clear and cheering a yellow every November as any tree. The Green Lake trees are probably too young to distinguish as to sex, but should any be female, they will make orange fruits which ripen in fall, with a stinking odor but edible nut-like seeds. Three Ginkgos are on the east side of the lake, by the children's play area northeast of the Evans Pool building; two others are in the Pitch n' Putt golf course. All are *gaunt*, which is normal for young trees of this species.

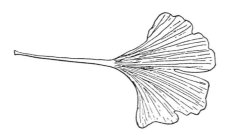

GOLDENCHAIN
Laburnum anagyroides

POISONOUS trees are not much in the news, since we tend not to eat them. Earlier, when people's diets consisted of more freshly harvested plant material, it was vital to avoid unsafe crops. Goldenchain, although in the pea family, and producing a little sort of bean- or pea-pod, is toxic. Despite this fact it has been widely planted beyond its European homeland. Now it comes up wild in Seattle. *Golden chains* of flowers are the reason for its popularity. They are abundant, pretty, and long lasting, appearing sometime between mid-April and early June. Aside from these plump, dangling treasures (which really do make the small trees seem to bend under the weight of their offering) the trees are ornamentally worthless. In the nursery trade they have been replaced by superior offerings.

Green Lake's 26 specimens are for the most part multitrunked, sprouty, and small. Perhaps only one is more than 30 feet tall. The unsightly, 2–3 inch seedpods persist for many months. Goldenchain's poor excuse for fall color would be funny if it wasn't so ugly.

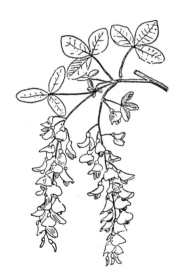

Alpine or Scotch GOLDENCHAIN
Laburnum alpinum

ALSO European, poisonous, and yellow-flowered, this species differs from common goldenchain in three ways: 1) it grows larger; 2) its flowers appear later and in longer clusters; 3) it is not silvery-hairy on its twigs and leaf undersides.

Far less abundant, it is at Green Lake in only two places: five are with six regular goldenchains in the bed of flowering cherries west of the Bathhouse Theatre. Two are on the southeast strip of shoreline north of 65th Street, and south of 67th. Another, formerly with this pair measured 30 feet tall in 1988; its trunk was just over 6 feet in circumference, and its spread of branches 26 feet wide, but it was cut down in May, 1990. The largest remaining is 25 feet tall, 4'8" around its trunk, and 23 feet wide.

GOLDEN RAIN TREE
Koelreuteria paniculata

MIXING UP "Goldenchain" and "Golden Rain" trees is as easy as slipping on ice. To keep the similar names straight, mnemonic tricks might be tried, but there are only two letters of difference between the names! Both trees bear yellow flowers. Fortunately, the scientific names and the trees themselves are utterly unrelated, and as dissimilar as can be.

Laburnum
-3 leaflets (like a clover)
-weak or nonexistent fall color
-pealike dripping clusters flowers
-flowers in May
-small, narrow, brownish, ugly seedpods
-young unfolding leaves silvery-green

Koelreuteria
-many leaflets
-bright orange or red fall color
-upright, open bunches of flowers
-flowers in summer or fall
-conspicuous bladder-like pods
-young leaves shrimp pink, bronzy

Both species reseed locally but only goldenchain is quite common wild. *Koelreuteria*, named after Joseph Gottlieb Koelreuter (1733–1806; a German natural history professor), is from China and Korea. Another name is Pride of India—sumptious sounding but applied to too many different kinds of trees. Because the Golden Rain Tree is so colorful, troublefree, and appropriately sized, we might express surprise that there are not more of them around. Why not remedy the matter and plant one yourself?

Green Lake has only thirteen, not counting wild offspring of seedling size. All are by the northwest parking lot. Largest is 42 feet tall, 5'4" around its trunk, and 32 feet wide. The thirteen are divided as follows: nine line the parking lot's long narrow planting bed, with kwanzan and other flowering cherries (not to mention numerous shrubs); four are in a bed with a holly beyond the parking lot, but near it, between Elm Hill and Oak Hill.

Autumn Glory HAWTHORN
Cratægus 'Autumn Glory'

HERE is still another case of Green Lake having only one specimen of a tree. In 1991 an Autumn Glory Hawthorn was planted at the park's northwest corner, by the gravel path opposite the gas station, near where Aurora intersects West Green Lake Way. Some cockspur and common hawthorns are also in the vicinity.

Green Lake's lone 'Autumn Glory' has a story behind it: Charles, Mary Ann, and William Fischer donated the tree as a memorial to their brother, Robert Light Fisher (1910–1989), a United Nations Administrator in the Middle East.

Like most hawthorns, Autumn Glory bears small white flowers; they open in mid-May to early June. The fruit or haws it forms are exceptionally shiny, large and beautiful red affairs in late autumn, hence its name. Like all haws, these are edible—to anyone who doesn't find them unpalatable. They can be as large as common table grapes. The tree resulted as a chance hybrid between an evergreen Mexican hawthorn and a European hawthorn. Ever since its introduction to the nursery trade in California 50 years ago, it has been lauded. But if you cherish spectacular fall leaf color, don't plant Autumn Glory Hawthorn: its leaves hang late, and are an uncooperative dingy yellow-green when they finally relinquish their hold in December. Fortunately the fruit is gorgeous, and the tree has few spines.

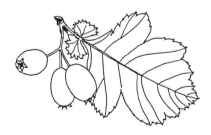

Cockspur HAWTHORN
Cratægus crus-galli

"THORNS," wrote P. J. Van Melle, an astute nurseryman, "that would gore a bull." If you like weaponry you'll love this tree. It is like a tree toothpick-factory. Carpenters need go no further if they seek no. 8 nails. Anyway, enough of this—since *thornless* versions can now be bought at nurseries, we should discuss the species' other attributes.

It is a small eastern North American tree, its top characteristically flattish, caused by widely-spreading branches that have little inclination to droop, and less to ascend. Dark, lustrous, spoonlike leaves are borne in dense quantity; in fall they turn amber and drop. During late May and early June, white flowers cover the tree. These give rise to round berries the size of small marbles, dull deep red upon maturity in October. Two big, hard, bony seeds are inside the yellow-fleshed berries.

Green Lake has 29, divided between 11 by the ballfields, and 18 at the north end of the lake extending from Aurora east nearly to Bagley Avenue.

Common HAWTHORN
Cratægus monogyna

EARTH's tallest hawthorn, as far as anyone has reported, is an individual of this species planted in Seattle's Volunteer Park at the direction of the Olmsted Brothers. In 1987 it measured 64 feet! Green Lake has 54 of these European hawthorns, and although none are so lofty, they too, were proposed on the landscape plans submitted by the famous landscape architects.

With little effort you may see why Common Hawthorn was so frequently planted. Year after year, without fail it smothers itself with blossoms in May, making a solid cloud of white or pink-tinted, odorous flowers. The only way to suppress its floral exuberance is to mal-prune it. Deep shade will also hamper it.

Red or purple-red haws, each containing one seed, are sometimes borne in sufficient quantity as to be showy in September. But generally this species is of no fall beauty, especially compared to eastern North American hawthorns. Its small leaves are cut into lobes, and are of no especial appeal to human eyes, and often attract aphids like a magnet. Short, sharp thorns like carpet tacks, guard the tree against larger animals. In brief, as a flowering tree it is supreme, but in other respects is about as exciting as an old shoe.

Paul's Scarlet HAWTHORN
Cratægus lævigata 'Paul's Scarlet'

WILLIAM Paul (1814–1905) of Waltham Cross, Hertfordshire, England, was a famous nurseryman who originated numerous gardenworthy plant varieties, including this hawthorn, more than 125 years ago. It differs from ordinary European hawthorns in having *deep pink-red* flowers composed of numerous petals rather than the customary five. Moreover, few haws or berries set, and they are wider than they are long, two- or three-seeded, and bright red. The tree is the same size and just as thorny and aphid-prone as common hawthorn.

Thousands are in Seattle, and stand out during May. But Green Lake has only one, planted by the children's play area northeast of the Evans Pool building.

Red HAWTHORN
Cratægus lævigata 'Punicea'

QUINTESSENTIALLY dark, the Red Hawthorns of Green Lake never fail to depress me. Yes, I admit to having a snobbish abhorrence of murky trees, so there is good reason to take these words with a hearty sprinkling of the proverbial salt. Red Hawthorns begin to leaf out in a pleasing manner, dispelling the gloom that had been their winter effect on the landscape. Then flowers the color of blood open in May, relieved, if viewed up close, by white in their centers. Small, deep green, high-gloss leaves soak up light all summer. A few unmemorable, firetruck-red berries are made; they are pea-sized and two-seeded. The leaves drop. Then the dense, intricately twisted, offensively twiggy crown sits and broods like a gigantic crow's nest. Long, skinny twigs reach out to snag passers-by. Yucch.

Green Lake's 27 Red Hawthorns are on the north side, from the east tennis courts all the way to the northwest near 76th Street. All are grafted, and the union between the lower trunk and upper portion is obvious. This variety has been marring landscapes since at least 1828.

English or Common HOLLY
Ilex Aquifolium

WINTERTIME cheer is holly's historic role. Even on the shortest day of the year, and the coldest, it maintains fresh, evergreen, handsome foliage, often set with sparkling berries. To endure wintry blasts and a full year's workload, the leaves are thick and tough. To escape the jaws of hungry animals, holly leaves are guarded with spines. People (clever beasts that we are) have not only managed to propagate spineless hollies, but have found bisexual specimens to grow, thus assuring ourselves a supply of good-looking berries without needing to plant females and males together. Dozens of holly varieties and hybrids exist, offering every desirable trait as to size, color and form. Green Lake's nine specimens, ahem, are all regular seedlings, not improved nursery stock. Though called English Holly, this species is native in much of Europe, north Africa and the mild parts of Asia. In Seattle it comes up wild all over the place. Birds can eat the berries that poison people.

European HORNBEAM
Carpinus Betulus

HARDWOOD cognoscenti and landscape architects may know this tree, but to most people it is merely a name—an unfamiliar name, at that. Probably the wood was likened to animal horn in its hardness. So reported John Gerard in his *Herball* of 1633: "in time it waxeth so hard that the toughnesse and hardnesse of it may be rather compared to horn than unto wood, and therefore it was called Hornbeam or hardbeam." George Emerson, writing much later (1850), rather thought the tree's trunk was "marked with longitudinal, irregular ridges, resembling the horns of animals of the deer kind." Additional explanations for the name exist.

Hornbeam is related to birches and alders, but is much more of a strong, woodland denizen than a pioneer of sunny, moist sites. Unlike its kindred, it reproduces even in shady forests. Sometimes a small tree, it usually grows as large as a house. The neatly scalloped, straight-veined leaves turn an adequate but not brilliant yellow in November. Pale green or yellowish catkins in spring give rise to distinctive clusters of winged seeds. Smooth, taut, dark gray bark covers a muscular-looking trunk. People plant hornbeams as woodland ornamentals, or as small to medium-sized shade trees for sites needing definite emphasis on finer, firmer texture. As long as its role of reserved presence is understood, hornbeam serves as an excellent tree, but to expect it to be a sumptuous beauty is to invite disillusionment.

Green Lake's example is two-trunked and grows in the Pitch n' Putt golf course, in an undistinguished shady margin near the west border, with 6 Norway spruces, 3 Norway maples and 7 Austrian pines.

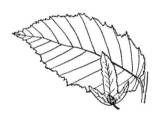

Common HORSE-CHESTNUT
Æsculus Hippocastanum

HOLDING a fresh horse-chestnut in your hand is a sensory thrill. It is so smooth, comfortably contoured, and seems ideal in size and weight. The contrast between the perfect, beautiful nut and its prickly, often discolored husk, adds to the pleasure. No wonder these big seeds are popular with children. The tree that drops these nuts every October, is a native of Greece, Albania and the Balkan region. As with some other trees whose native land is of small extent, the Horse-chestnut has shown no hesitation about thriving wherever we plant it; now even wild ones frequently come up in our area, often from nuts planted by squirrels. The tree has been immensely popular, growing to a huge shade tree that outclasses most other trees of equal stature by bearing splendid large flower clusters during late April and early May. The succeeding nuts, although so big, abundant and pretty, are poisonous. Thus Loudon, author of the greatest book about trees ever, suggested that "the manner in which it scatters its flowers on the grass, and the comparative uselessness of its fruit and timber, make it an excellent emblem of ostentation."

Horse-chestnut is unlike the edible or sweet chestnut trees (*Castanea* species; not at Green Lake) in every way, except that the nuts of both are large, brown, and encased in prickly husks. Edible chestnut husks are densely covered with needlelike barbs; horse-chestnut husks are scantily clad with stout short prickles.

This species has about the most fascinating leafbuds of any. An early spring treat is to watch the huge, varnished buds swell, burst and erupt to unfold their soft greenery, coated with rich orange fuzz.

Green Lake has one Horse-chestnut with zelkova trees on the east beach. Five younger ones are with the numerous black walnuts at the southwest part of the lake.

Red HORSE-CHESTNUT
Æsculus × carnea

HYBRIDIZE common horse-chestnut with red buckeye (*Æsculus Pavia*, a shrubby southeastern U.S. species, not at Green Lake) and the result is Red Horse-chestnut. Unlike most hybrids, this one is fertile and can reproduce itself by seed. It is smaller, darker, and rather more gouty that the common horse-chestnut, besides bearing smaller, rather deep pink flowers that open a bit later, and browner nut-husks with fewer prickles. Both its parental species appeal to me more.

Green Lake's lone example is with the park's only yellow buckeye, northeast of the Pitch n' Putt golf course.

Rocky Mountain JUNIPER
Juniperus scopulorum

DURING 1991 someone planted three tall, silvery junipers with two vine maples in a bed in the Pitch n' Putt golf course. The intent of such a combination escapes me utterly, and to judge from the wet soil there, it would seem a scheme designed to struggle if it survives at all. The trees in question are both first-rate ornamentals, and thrive in our climate, but their use together in a crowded planting-bed in a soggy golf course, is about like adding whole pineapples to your mixed salad—you can certainly *do* it, and temporarily have a striking conversation piece, but it *won't work*. Junipers, whether shrubs or trees, should be planted in the sunniest, driest, best-drained sites. Green Lake is not a good site for junipers, and the golf course, with its acidic muck, is particularly bad.

There are 21 different varieties of Rocky Mountain Juniper presently for sale in North American nurseries, exclusive of its shrubby versions. The exact varietal identity of the Green Lake trio is unknown to me. They are strongly upright, silvery-gray, and about as exhilarating to smell as any tree in the park. The species is noteworthy not only for having many varied garden forms and a penetrating fragrance, but also in having a vast North American range, growing from high mountains to sea-level, from groundcover size to trees 78 feet tall.

European LARCH
Larix decidua

SIXTY-SIX European Larches are at Green Lake: it is the 12th most abundant tree at the park. These conifers, like bald cypress and dawn redwood, drop their needles in winter. The needles are about an inch long, and turn yellow before falling. Cones, 1–2⅛ inches long, stay attached to the twigs instead of dropping. Not only does the larch mark the seasons more emphatically than evergreen conifers, it also has a softer visual impact than its kindred spruces and firs. Its wood, though, is comparatively hard. North Americans call related trees by the lovely Indian names Tamarack or Hackmatack.

Since Green Lake has so many, a few of the largest should be singled out. On the southeast lakeshore, near the giant sepulchral weeping willow north of 63rd Street, is a grove of five larches, one of which is the park's tallest, 75 feet or so, with its trunk 7 feet around.

The stoutest European Larch in all of Seattle is in the Pitch n' Putt golf course, 8¼ feet around its swollen trunk, its branches shading over 60 feet of ground.

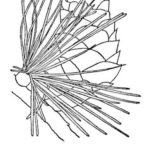

Japanese LARCH
Larix Kaempferi

VERY similar to European Larch, the "Kara-matsu" differs in having wider, bluish-green (not yellow-green) needles; squat, blunter, shorter cones with recurved scales; and pinkish instead of beige twigs. Its fall color is earlier and brighter. Green Lake has only six, in a grove with two European larches, near the middle of the northwest parking lot. The two Europeans are the *tall* tree in the middle, and the *stout-trunked, leaning* one on the highest point of ground. The rest are Japanese Larches.

Black LOCUST
Robinia Pseudoacacia

PEOPLE love real character, or *distinctiveness to a memorable degree.* Black Locust obliges powerfully. It is one of those trees that most of us know, if not by name, then by sight. Although originally native to a restricted portion of the eastern U.S., it has been one of the planet's most extensively grown trees, and has joyfully run wild by seed and root-sucker in most places where it has been introduced.

Probably Black Locust's most singular feature is its dark, deeply corrugated trunk, and rugged crown of thorny branches. Even in winter, bereft of summer verdure, its silhouette against the sky is a sight to make us pause in admiration, like viewing a painting and feeling we cannot help looking, being held by an invisible bond, and told to "look deep, look long." When summer beckons forth locust's greenery, the tree responds with a flourish worthy of any painter's brush. The tender, soft, gently fluttering leaflets of grass green color, become background to May and June flowers, creamy white, sweet, and irresistible to bees. Through the heat of July and August, locust maintains its green, airy composure, not, as do so many weaker species, becoming pale and yellow or gray tinged from the stress. Then in autumn, the flat seedpods 2–5 inches long, begin to fall with the leaves. Locust is no tree to see at this time of year, however—with all its other traits combining to make a unique, stare-you-in-the-eye presence, its fall "color" is amazingly dreadful.

Green Lake has two on the east bathing beach, with zelkova trees. They lean apart from one another. A third, of uncompromised aloneness, reigns on the southeast strip of the shore, north of Kirkwood Place, south of 63rd Street. It forks low into two, leans away from the lake, and looks like it could split or fall all the way over any minute.

Globe LOCUST
Robinia Pseudoacacia 'Umbraculifera'

TAKE a mighty tree of any kind, and you will find that in cultivation, sooner or later, dwarf offspring come about. Black Locust's bushy, trunkless form, not content to be of reduced size, also lacks flowers and thorns. So it is grown grafted high upon a locust trunk, to be a lollipop or globe-headed little tree. After decades, the roundness of the crown becomes broader than tall, and eventually a fair-sized umbrella-like shape is achieved. That is, unless someone clips the branches periodically to force the tree into permanent dwarfhood. Green Lake has two by the caretaker's building near 77th Street at the north end of the park.

Evergreen MAGNOLIA
Magnolia grandiflora

VOLUPTUOUS beauties, these are Reubensesque heart-throbs of the tree world. Large and hardy, they have been praised lushly and planted globally. Evergreen Magnolia is a southern U.S. native, symbolizing well the sultry wealth of warm vegetation. It grows as an immense forest tree and is sawn into lumber like any other hardwood. What makes it so special ornamentally is its giant, glossy, *plastic-like* evergreen leaves, which are often enhanced by attractive reddish-brown fuzz on their undersides. Against this rich greenery are set giant waxy white flowers of entrancing fragrance, borne all summer long, one after another, instead of all at once like those of most magnolias. Its foliage is as tropically resplendent as that of any house plant, but it endures freezing. Never a rose without a thorn, Evergreen Magnolia's "blemish" is that its spent petals turn brown, and they *and* the fallen leaves are messy.

Green Lake has five youngsters planted around a Japanese snowbell tree in the traffic island north of the Evans Pool building.

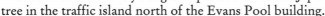

Star MAGNOLIA
Magnolia stellata

BRIGHT white flowers richly fragrant and profusely borne, make Star Magnolia light up the landscape in March. After the flowers finish, leaves follow, and the beauty is gone until next year, since the twiggy summer foliage does not reignite our enthusiasm with anything approaching a satisfying fall coloration. In winter the large, felty flowerbuds are interesting.

Star Magnolia is a small shrubby tree from Japan, recognized by having flowers with 12 to 18 finger-like petals, which can be pink, though they are normally so white as to appear bleached. Anyone who doesn't believe that it can attain treehood is invited to observe one at 808 36th Avenue East, 26 feet tall with a trunk more than 8 inches thick.

Green Lake has two, both dating from 1991. The first is at the northwest corner of the park, with a freshly planted but likely doomed white fir, three older sawara cypresses and four zebra cedars. The second Star Magnolia is on the southeast strip of shoreline east of 65th Street. It was planted in memory of Chan Chilton by the Northwest District of the Seattle Parks Department, and is with two young white firs, by a grove of eight large, old maples. (Near this second Star Magnolia, someone stuck in three pussy willow twigs in late February 1992—they *may* grow into trees.)

Bigleaf MAPLE
Acer macrophyllum

HUMONGOUS size sets this maple apart. Hundreds of maple species beautify the earth, but none are bigger. Washington's tallest was 158 feet in 1988, and trunks boasting 35 feet in circumference are on record. Leaves larger than dinner plates are common. The flower clusters lengthen to as long as 9 inches, anytime from mid-March through early May, scenting the air with nectar-rich little yellow flowers. The seeds are winged, bristly brown affairs.

Bigleaf Maple is Seattle's most abundant tree. Its fall color varies from year to year, though generally is about like that of a hamburger bun crust. In the best years it is bright, glowing gold.

Green Lake supports only 18, not counting seedlings. Most, including the largest, grow on the southeast strip from 63rd to 67th Street. A colossus near the restrooms measures more than 14 feet in girth—or if you prefer: its trunk is 4½ feet thick. The largest leaf I found was 16½ inches long and 21½ inches wide, on a stalk over a foot long. Larger leaves have been found by other leaf-hunters.

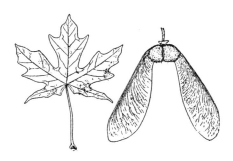

English MAPLE
Acer campestre

HARD wood, but leaves of soft outline and color, typify the English hedge maple. Its leaves are bluntish and small for a maple, about the size of a Ritz cracker. In November they turn butter yellow. The winged seeds are borne in widely diverging pairs. This species performs to perfection in our region.

Green Lake's lone English Maple is north of the wading pool. Three-trunked, it reaches out from under the repressive influence of two large birches; before it spreads a groundcover planting of prickly yellow-flowered broom. To look at this maple's reduced stature, you would scarcely believe there are majestically larger ones elsewhere in western Washington. But it is small for good reason: observe how many trees and shrubs are jammed together in this spot; imagine how their roots must compete for moisture. The maple at least gets light, which the pines behind it surely long for.

Japanese MAPLE
Acer palmatum

NOVEMBER leaf color as thrilling as any floral display in spring, is Japanese Maple's sign of glory. An unlimited life-giving spectrum of flaring colors is able to banish all cold, dismal associations. Yellow, orange and red in every shade and depth, blaze forth according to the variety. People who have not experienced the potency of these colors before, gasp merrily when first seeing them. Even if we were color-blind, we would still enjoy these small, gentle, delicate trees, for their well-balanced branching habit and leaf arrangement.

Green Lake has few. Three are hidden in somber woods north of the Pitch n' Putt golf course, with 22 companion Norway spruces and some dull sycamore maples. An ecstatic *purpleleaf* one is on the fieldhouse patio, in a large square planter-box edged by a bench.

Norway MAPLE
Acer platanoides

TOUGH, strong, solid, and opportunistic, Norway Maple is like a teenage athlete. These qualities have made it one of the most frequently planted trees in downtown urban cores. If healthy stock is planted properly, then it pulses with vigor and grows apace, be the soil ever so poor, the air ever so polluted. If you find a stunted Norway Maple, surely it was planted too deep, or with girdling roots, or has been the victim of a rare degree of soil-compaction or other stifling influence.

Clean-looking, sharply lobed leaves about the size of a hand with fingers outspread, produce a full leafy canopy. In autumn, the large, very flat seed-pairs are noteworthy for their conspicuous pallor, and wings pointing in opposite directions. The leaf color change is late and usually yellow, sometimes orange on trees growing in dry locations.

Over 30 cultivated varieties exist in this country, and the species is naturalized in Seattle. It reproduces better in woods than do our native maples.

Green Lake has 86 Norway Maples, and some of them are the **'Schwedleri'** variety, which could not be distinguished when I counted the trees in December. 'Schwedleri', unlike typical Norway Maples, unfolds spring leaves that are reddish-purple. They look very regal in April, then gradually fade to a duller, heavy bronze-green. In fall its color is also deeper, being rosy-orange, never mere yellow. Some 'Schwedleri' can be seen by the fieldhouse. Green Lake's largest regular Norway Maple is on the northwest shore, right by West Green Lake Drive somewhat north of 76th Street; its hefty trunk is almost ten feet in circumference.

Sycamore MAPLE
Acer Pseudoplatanus

MAKE sure to not confuse Sycamore Maple with Sycamore tree—see PLANETREE for the latter. Only three trees are more abundant at Green Lake than the 92 Sycamore Maples: Douglas fir numbers 110, bald cypress 102, and kwanzan cherry 95. Therefore, since it is hopelessly common, despite its being a boring tree, everyone who loves the park's trees must accept it.

In Europe (its original home), Sycamore Maple is the premier forest maple, living for centuries, sometimes attaining monumental dimensions and thereby achieving a grand appearance that generates affectionate respect. Transplanted to Seattle's gravelly-clay excuse for soil, especially when the organic layer or topsoil is missing, and the subsoil compacted, Sycamore Maple sulks. Rightly so; its roots find too little nourishment. The dry summers it endures rather than accepts without complaint. In brief: it grows more slowly. Slow growth, admittedly, is not necessarily a problem in trees: often it is exactly what people desire. But Sycamore Maple is so colorless and unassuming that it should be planted chiefly as a background shade tree—not used as a major component of landscape ringing a city's prize park. Very rarely do Sycamore Maples turn a pleasing color in fall, but what a sight for sore eyes that is when it occurs: a barely believable clear, lemon-yellow from top to bottom!

The leaves are a heartless depth of green on top, but mercifully paler beneath: when they flutter in the wind the contrast is delightful. A sort of thick, wrinkly texture distinguishes them from most other maple leaves. Nor are they sharply pointed, preferring an obtuse, muted outline. Just as Norway maple has its Schwedler variety, Sycamore Maple has its **Wineleaf** variation, known as 'Atropurpureum' (or 'Spaethii'): its summer leaves are pink-purplish on their undersides. Green Lake has many Wineleaf Maples.

Norway and Sycamore maples can be recognized by bark alone. Norway's is like that of bigleaf maple; Sycamore Maple has smooth to flaky, rather than furrowed trunks, often beige in color instead of pure gray.

On Elm Hill southwest of the Bathhouse Theatre is a Sycamore Maple atop the highest point of ground, whose trunk *split* partly but has partly welded itself back together, making a curiosity—you can look *through* the trunk. In the vicinity of the wading pool, the park's largest Sycamore Maple measures 8½ feet around—among Seattle's biggest.

Vine MAPLE
Acer circinatum

Two little Vine Maples were planted with Rocky Mountain junipers in the Pitch n' Putt golf course in 1991. Otherwise, Green Lake has none of these natives. The golf course pair are not worth going out of your way to visit, but since the species is common in Seattle it deserves a fair write-up here.

To begin with, it is *not* a vine, but rather a slender, usually multitrunked small tree. Yet in moist, mossy woods, its elongated, snaky limbs and trunks can tangle in vine-like complexity. Yellow is its forest fall color; exposed to the sun, Vine Maple grows bushier, denser, and colors reddish. Even were its fall color less beautiful, it would still be welcome in woodland gardens because of its smooth, skin-like, greenish bark; and easily integrated texture and scale.

The only problem is its resentment of pruning. Few trees look so marred and respond so poorly to having branches removed. Thus, it is ideally planted where plenty of room exists for it to grow very large, unmolested. Or perhaps it should be periodically cut back to the ground and allowed to resprout. It requires at least 10 feet of width and height, and there are many very much larger examples—at most over 60 feet tall.

MOUNTAIN ASH
Sorbus aucuparia

ITALY'S flag of green, white and red might just as well symbolize this tree, which is quite as colorful with leaves, flowers and berries. But glowing orange fall color belongs to the tree alone. It is mainly the bright berries and fall foliage that endear Mountain Ash to us. Its April-May flowers are indeed pretty, but not as outstanding as other tree flowers or as flashy as the Mountain Ash's own autumn show.

Sorbus is a large genus of trees, and though most hail from the Old World, even high-elevation Washington has native mountain ashes. Yet in Seattle, the European species is seen over 99% of the time. Its beauty led to extensive planting, and its berries' attractiveness to robins and other birds led to its becoming wild here. Most of these trees are 25 to 40 feet tall. The bark is reminiscent of cherry or birch bark, in its polished, horizontal, peeling way.

Green Lake has 2 8 regular European Mountain Ashes (also known as Rowan trees), plus three with extraordinarily big berries, measuring as much as ⅝ of an inch wide. The regular trees are scattered about the park; the big-berried ones grow only on the northeast shore, one by three bald cypresses south of Meridian Avenue; two, much smaller, by the lake to the westward, south of Orin Court. If taste could kill, these attractive fruits might do it, but they are not poisonous.

Black OAK
Quercus velutina

UTILITY rather than beauty is the special strength of Black Oak. Compared to its associates (red, scarlet and pin oaks) of eastern North America, it is less lovely but possibly more useful. Not only does it supply wood (which is admittedly not the best), the Black Oak was widely employed in dyeing wool, silk and other materials. A yellow-orange substance obtained from its inner bark was named quercitron. Sometimes, the tree was known as Yellow Oak or Dyer's Oak. In leather tanning it was highly esteemed.

Ornamentally, on the other hand, it is a rough, coarse tree, with large, thick, dark leaves, that are scurfy with fuzz in spring before shining in the summer. Its bark is chunky, deep gray or blackish. Overall, people prefer oaks that are brighter or more elegant—and most are, in fact.

Green Lake has one Black Oak, in the oak collection north of the Pitch n' Putt golf course. It is the middle tree north of the path, with a larger swamp white oak west of it, and a much smaller bur oak northeastward.

Bur OAK
Quercus macrocarpa

BRAWNY, big and hairy, Bur Oak rarely becomes a large, pleasing tree when planted in Seattle, far from its midwest and eastern U.S. homeland. Probably most of them planted here are dissatisfied with the lack of summer heat and moisture, and find the soils nowhere near as deep and rich as they're accustomed to. Few of their giant acorns are produced, which are never so large here as in the wild. Since the species offers no fall color worth mentioning, and its form is comparatively stunted here, few have been planted—and no more need be. Big, deeply lobed leaves with trademark waists are distinctive, dark on top, whitish underneath.

Green Lake has three on Oak Hill (by the northwest parking lot). The westernmost is in a shrub bed with *Spiræa* × *Van Houttei* and *Forsythia*. A fourth Bur Oak is in the oak collection north of the Pitch n' Putt golf course. It is north of the path, and smaller than the nearby black and swamp white oaks. What I think may be a bur oak/white oak hybrid is south of the path—see White OAK, p 121.

Daimyo OAK
Quercus dentata

GREEN LAKE'S lone Daimyo Oak is perfectly amazing. Flawless, symmetrical, healthy, and larger than any other known on the West Coast, it is the kind of thing usually only dreamed of by tree lovers. Biased as I am, it ill behooves me to speak of these things, but my heart has been so charmed by this oak that I'll venture to suggest that even people who dislike trees might, if showed this East Asian marvel, gulp and concede it a goodly sight and worthy of being seen often. Maybe not, though: William Blake sighed "The tree which moves some to tears of joy is in the eyes of others only a green thing which stands in the way."

Its leaves are larger than those of most oaks, measuring up to 15 inches long and 10 inches wide. Numerous finger-like lobes fringe them. They turn a pink-tawny color in fall. The acorns are in unusual bristly cups. The bark is light-colored and rugged in oak fashion.

The Daimyo Oak is the largest oak north of the Pitch n' Putt golf course; when measured in 1988 it stood 70 feet tall, 62 feet wide, its trunk 8'7½" around.

Oriental White OAK
Quercus aliena var. *acuteserrata*

THIS tree has proved *a dud* in Seattle. Every one of the handful known in this city is boring at best, but usually ugly. The Green Lake pair are about the worst of the lot. Surely there is something here that they suffer from, because in their East Asian homeland they are not considered sickly eyesores.

The 4–7 inch leaves are in the chestnut oak class, rather sharp with 10 to 17 shallow teeth on each side. Disease blotches usually mar the leaf surface. Underneath they are covered with inconspicuous, close, dense fuzz. Their fall color is, like that of horse-chestnut, yellowish-brown. The acorns, ripening in October, are almost never made here and are nothing special.

The two smallest of the oaks north of the Pitch n' Putt golf course are Oriental White Oaks. Both are south of the path and flank the giant daimyo Oak.

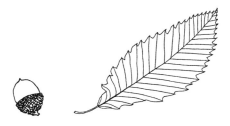

Pin OAK
Quercus palustris

SLENDERNESS is Pin Oak's mark. As a fondue fork is to a regular table fork, or a greyhound to other dogs, so is this to oaks. If it were merely lean, we would admire its fine, delicate outlines. But it also has glossy leaves that turn bright red in fall. Since it complements its decorativeness with strength and ease of transplanting, Pin Oak has been widely planted far beyond its central and eastern U.S. range. It rejoices in Seattle, growing very large and coloring in fall as well as any oak. One of its drawbacks bothers some people—the leaves often hang brown and dead on the twigs until nearly spring.

Green Lake has three with two white firs in the traffic island north of the Evans Pool building. Two are on Oak Hill (by the northwest parking lot) with four scarlet oaks, four red oaks, and three bur oaks.

Red OAK
Quercus rubra

MASSIVE is the best word to describe Red Oak. Its bulky, swollen trunk and limbs grow enormous, bearing a branching head sometimes spreading more than 125 feet wide, full of leaves at least the size of bricks, at most measuring as large as 14½ inches long and 9 inches wide. Fat roundish acorns dwarf most others. In short, it might be called Big Oak as well as Red Oak. The bark is relatively smooth for an oak, and the leaves are a tad dull, and not as vibrant in autumn as those of the related scarlet and pin oaks. In fact, some Red Oaks have the yellowish-brown fall color typically associated with black oak.

This species is the original Red Oak, also called the Common, Eastern, or Northern Red Oak. Other red oaks have qualifying names such as Shumard red oak or Southern red oak, etc.

Green Lake has four on Oak Hill; seven youngsters are in a row on the southwest shore, on the lake side of the path.

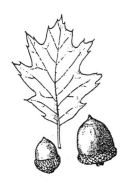

Scarlet OAK
Quercus coccinea

 INTERMEDIATE between stout red oak and thin pin oak, the Scarlet Oak is more commonly confused with pin oak. In fall it is deeper-colored and justly famous for it. In summer, its leaves, shaped like those of pin oak but bigger, are without the conspicuous tiny patches of tawny hairs in the vein axils that characterize pin oak leaves. In winter, note that the leafbuds are hairy, and the trunk is rougher barked. It is as hard to say which of these species is a superior ornamental as it can be to differentiate the two. Since pin oak can be twiggy and cluttered, but Scarlet Oak almost never is, the latter has an edge. But the city's finest pin oaks please me as much as do any of the Scarlet Oaks. It's a close call, maybe a draw. Scarlet Oak has been less commonly planted, but this has more to do with its transplantability than its ornamental value.

 Green Lake has four on Oak Hill, with four red oaks, two pin oaks, and the wholly dissimilar bur oak trio. Crowding among these trees has resulted in a loss of some of their characteristic shape, since they're all struggling for sunlight.

Swamp White OAK
Quercus bicolor

THE shallowly lobed leaves of Swamp White Oak are glossy green on top, pale and felty underneath—unquestionably a joy to gaze at and to handle. But the tree's flaky bark looks sloppy; its tendency to form a crude, twiggy, flattish crown, and its usually ordinary yellow fall color, condemn it to the discard heap. For wet sites it may be planted with advantage. It comes from the northern half of the central and eastern U.S., and extreme southern Canada near the Great Lakes.

Green Lake has one exceptionally handsome Swamp White Oak north of the Pitch n' Putt golf course, north of the path, 64 feet tall, 55 feet wide, its trunk 6'1" around (as of 1988)—larger than the black oak east of it.

White OAK
Quercus alba

PALE ashy-white bark caused this eastern North American tree to be called White Oak. Magnificent stature, great abundance and valuable wood, as well as stately beauty, made it a general favorite back East. Among famous and historic trees there are more White Oaks than any other kind of tree. This species is the standard by which other species in the white oak group are judged.

The leaves are smooth, gently lobed without bristly points, and are pink in spring, rosy in October.

Green Lake has one north of the Pitch n' Putt golf course, at the east end of the oaks south of the path. Next to it is a bigger hybrid oak, possibly a cross of White Oak and bur oak (called *Quercus × Bebbiana*). The hybrid is sometimes sickly.

Chinese PHOTINIA
Photinia serrulata

WHETHER or not to include this east Asian broadleaf evergreen in the book posed some pondering, but despite the fact that the park's lone example is a bit small, I decided to include it. After all, it is worthwhile to remind everyone that some plants are too awkwardly large to be called shrubs, yet suspiciously small to be granted title to full treehood. Chinese Photinia is an excellent example. It was certainly thought to be a shrub when introduced to cultivation in the West. But some specimens in our gardens and parks have grown more than 40 feet tall, so we must consider it at least a potential tree.

The Green Lake tree, two-trunked, is on the fieldhouse patio, right in a corner by the door. Its leaves are holly-green and lined with fine little teeth. In March and April, brownish-bronze colored new leaves unfold, soon followed by white flowers in rather large clusters. Red berries may also ripen. A member of the rose family, Photinia is related to hawthorns, cotoneasters, pyracantha, mountain ashes, etc.

Austrian Black PINE
Pinus nigra

RUGGED, hard, stout branches bearing thick masses of luxurious dark green 3–5½ inch needles, make this common pine a conspicuous sight. Since it is wholly hardy, people have planted it far beyond its native land. Growing large, it becomes one of the darkest, densest and coarsest of all trees. The bark is thick, scaly and unremarkable. The pale cones measure 2½ to 4 inches long, with minute spines. If a pine is needed to stand up to adversity and neglect, even abuse—the Austrian is a safe choice. If a beautiful pine is desired, choose another species

Green Lake has 25. Three are worth singling out: first, a big multitrunked specimen overlooking the ballfields from a rise; second, one that children enjoy climbing is all by itself on the lake's southeast strip north of 67th Street; third, one very near the water's edge by the wading pool's outlet stream.

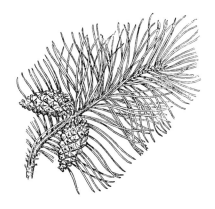

Chinese PINE
Pinus tabulæformis

THIS little known Chinese cousin differs from the ubiquitous Austrian black pine in being less regularly shaped, smaller, less dense, and in having paler and squatter cones, only 1½ to 2½ inches long. The needles vary in length but are approximately the same as those of the Austrian species. In short: it is less drably formal. Also called Chinese Red Pine, it sometimes has reddish bark, which unfortunately is never so pronounced as on Japanese red and Scots pines. Not an overpowering brute like Austrian pine, it can be safely planted in small yards, though it will still be harsh and nondescript unless artfully pruned.

There are eighteen at Green Lake. One is with six Oriental spruces north of the Bathhouse Theatre. Seven (with 12 Scots and 6 Japanese red pines) are between the northwest tennis courts and the main path. Ten are on the west shore between 70th and 71st Streets.

Eastern White PINE
Pinus Strobus

    WHITE pines in general differ from black and red pines by being bluish-green, softer in appearance, and in making lighter-weight wood. There are different botanic details, too, such as needles clustered in fives instead of pairs and triplets. As landscape ornamentals, however, white pines are valued above all for their *light color*. They are not literally white, any more than any people are, but when you see one next to a red or black pine, you instantly apprehend the aptness of the name, even as you imbibe the beauty of the tree. Their effect on the eye is like the tones of a harp on the ear; black and red pines in contrast are definitely of the brass or percussion section of instruments.

    Eastern White Pine is the original white pine, native primarily in the central and eastern U.S., with Canadian and Central American outposts. Until upstaged by Douglas fir early in this century, it was North America's most important evergreen lumber tree. No tree east of the Mississippi River grows taller. It holds its long, broad boughs horizontally, and the pliable 3 to 5½ inch needles coat the tree thinly, letting sunlight pierce through to reflect off the smoothish, pitchy, deep gray trunk. Banana-like curved cones are sticky with pitch, 4 to 8 inches long, brown when fully ripe and open.

    Green Lake has 53, from near the northwest tennis courts to the west strip of the lake north of 68th Street.

125

Himalayan White PINE *hybrid*
Pinus Wallichiana hybrid

This hybrid is the only one of its kind I have ever seen. It grows north of the Bathhouse Theatre, in a row with six prim Oriental spruces, three Japanese red pines, three Lawson cypresses, and a Chinese pine. The unique hybrid is distinguished from these solemn green neighbors in its having the customary pretty bluish color that marks all species of white pines.

This specimen differs from nonhybrid Himalayan white pines, in having shorter needles and cones, and hairy twigs.

Japanese Black PINE
Pinus Thunbergiana

Unlike Austrian black pine, the "Kuro-matsu" is wayward in its growth, almost always having a bent trunk and informal habit. It is also smaller, as well as having slightly shorter needles (3 to 5 inches long), and cones (1½ to 3 inches). More obviously, its buds, especially in their elongating "candle" stage in early spring, are vividly white with hairs, prettily contrasting with the green needles.

Green Lake has just four, by the yellow buckeye and red horsechestnut northeast of the Pitch n' Putt golf course. Two much smaller Austrian black pines are also nearby.

Japanese Red PINE
Pinus densiflora

REDDISH bark sets both this species and Scots pine apart. Green Lake has 90 of the Asian and 91 of the European, so plenty of both are there for you to compare. Japanese red pine is more frequently multitrunked than any other pine grown hereabouts. The needles, 3 to 5 inches long, are usually rather widely spaced, on very slender, pale twigs. Cones 1½ to 3 inches long are not distinctive.

Known as "Aka-matsu" in Japan, it is also native in China and Korea. The romantically picturesque crown, perched upon reddish trunks, is what makes this small to mid-sized pine popular. Tanyosho pine (treated on page 132) is one of its variations.

Mountain PINE
Pinus uncinata

GIANT Mugo Pine is an alternate name for this. Like the mugo pine, it resides on mountains in Europe. Dark to a ghastly extent, short-needled, with inconspicuous little brown cones, it is as homely and little deserving of cultivation for ornament as any pine.

Green Lake may have one Mountain Pine. The four-trunked specimen north of the fieldhouse in the grassy median strip of the parking lot (otherwise planted with five Norway maples) may be a mugo pine, but it has the *cones* of a Mountain Pine, despite its less than fully treelike habit. Perhaps it is a hybrid. Going towards the lake you can see five typical shrubby mugo pines around a shirotae cherry in a planter.

Mugo PINE
Pinus Mugo

MUGO Pine, from European mountains, is *shrubby* with rare exceptions. The biggest one I've ever seen happens to be in the Pitch n' Putt golf course. Note that Mugo Pine is usually a rockery plant, a low little bush little taller than a groundcover juniper. People step on them. Some of this form are at Green Lake north of the fieldhouse, but I didn't count them as "trees." However, the golf course has a 19 foot tall, two-trunked behemoth that spreads 42 feet wide, its trunk 1¼ feet through! This is the equivalent, say, of an African violet four feet wide. Three smaller, but still big, Mugo Pines are in the golf course, as are four shaded ones just outside the fence, facing the parking lot. Mugo Pine needles are 1 to 3 inches long, and the cones ¾ to 1½ inches. Mountain pine (treated above) is identical except treelike, with bigger, *heavier* cones. The two species commonly hybridize, and likely Green Lake has an intermediate race.

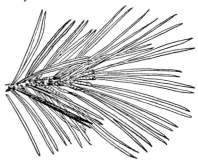

Ponderosa PINE
Pinus ponderosa

BULL Pine is not a glamorous name, but it captures perfectly the spirit of this tree. As a bull is muscular, stout, big and strong, so is Ponderosa Pine. Look at the six east of the Aqua Theatre and you'll agree. Their bolt-upright trunks, plump twigs radiating 5 to 10 inch needles, seem to proclaim sturdy vigor. Youthful now, in decades to come this grove should be of landmark magnitude.

Ponderosa Pine is native to much of western North America, including parts of Washington. It's way too big for average yards in cities, but makes a grand, tall subject wherever room permits. It is easily recognized by its straight, massive trunk, long needles borne in trios, and prickly, light-weight cones.

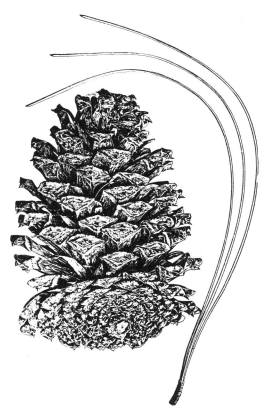

Red PINE
Pinus resinosa

AMERICAN Red Pine might be a better name for this tree, lest it be confused with the far more commonly grown Japanese red pine. Native to the Great Lakes area and eastward, it was once called Norway pine, either because it was abundant near the town of Norway, Maine, or because of some real or imagined connection to Norway spruce timber.

There is just one Red Pine at Green Lake, by the wading pool outlet stream stone bridge, and it is ideally representative of the species at maturity in our region: its trunk is slender, branchless below, and somewhat reddish though not to the unmistakable extent of Japanese red, or Scots pines. The needles are dark olive green, 4 to 7 inches long, in pairs, hiding cones only 1 to 2½ inches long. A peculiarity of the needles is that even while they are still fresh and green, you can *break* them cleanly by bending them, whereas most pine needles are so limber they can be twisted back and tied in loops. Try it if you can find any on the ground.

The tree is a regular, utterly average pine, of no surpassing beauty. Yet when *young* it was an Adonis. This species' beauty when Christmas-tree sized is exceptional, so until it grows big and makes many cones, losing its youthful force, it is an elegant, colorful, and shapely tree. Some people also love it when it forms forests of reddish trunks in Wisconsin and Michigan, but that is beside the point if we are discussing the tree's role in ornamental landscape usage. As people prefer kittens to cats, too bad we cannot hold back the clock with Red Pine—the contrast between its youth and old age is painfully striking.

Scots PINE
Pinus sylvestris

ORANGE-RED bark and unconventional sage-green needles are this tree's identifying features. Compared to Japanese red pine, which sometimes has bark so similar that you cannot tell the two apart by bark alone, Scots Pine has denser, stiffer, paler, shorter needles, ranging from 1 to 4½ inches; cones 1¼ to 3 inches, which drop more readily than those of its Japanese cousin; and a tendency to grow tall and straight, with a single trunk.

Green Lake has 91, and unfortunately most look unhealthy, with shorter needles and less annual growth than they could be producing. Since the species ranges from Scotland to the Pacific Ocean, perhaps a *poor strain* was planted at Green Lake, where nearly all are on the west side, from the Bathhouse Theatre to the Aqua Theatre. Three are in a bed of St. John's-wort groundcover and shrubby mugo pines southwest of the east parking lot, near the fieldhouse.

Shore PINE
Pinus contorta

SALTWATER shores of the Pacific Northwest are the home of this native pine. It can be small and shrubby or soar to 100 feet in height. Either way, inordinate *needle density* characterizes it. Collecting snow and blocking wind, Shore Pines blew down in multitudes in the destructive December 1990 storm. In landscape work its best role is as an undemanding evergreen screen. Its paired, 1 to 3 inch needles are brighter green and better-looking than those of the swarthy mugo or mountain pines. Its cones are very small, each scale tipped by a tiny prickle.

Green Lake's 16 are all on the narrow west side, striving to block out the blight of traffic on Aurora. They are certainly the right choice as to mass and size. An inland, montane form of this species, known as **Lodgepole Pine**, is much taller and less dense; it would not serve as usefully in such a site.

Tanyosho PINE
Pinus densiflora 'Umbraculifera'

MUSHROOM-SHAPED, compact, dwarf, sometimes appropriately called Japanese Tabletop or Umbrella Pine, this is altogether different from the routine Japanese red pine—from which it derives. Green Lake's eight Tanyosho Pines are on the southeast shore, between Sunnyside and 67th Street. Small now, eventually they may grow more than 30 feet tall, and be wider still.

Hybrid PLANE or SYCAMORE
Platanus × hybrida

THIS is a whale of a tree, truly of monstrous size. Crossing the largest deciduous tree of eastern North America (Sycamore) with the largest of Asia Minor (Oriental Planetree), results in offspring of unparalleled gusto, growing in fifty years to look as if a century old, and when at the 100-year mark, still rapidly increasing in bulk, fully healthy—even in sites that prove difficult for most trees to endure. In brief, hybrid planes are like comic-book superheroes in their speed, strength and seeming invulnerability.

Different clones of the cross have been selected, named and propagated. Most famous is **London Plane**. Green Lake has no London Planes, mostly having the husky clone 'Pyramidalis'. The trunks are hugely swollen, and almost always flake off their darker outer bark scales to reveal yellow-green, thinner, younger patches—an unmistakable point of identification.

Broad, maple-shaped leaves, shallowly lobed and very short-stalked, are covered in spring with "lint-like" hairs that drift away to the annoyance of breathing animals. Pale brown seedballs 1–2 inches wide dangle in loose array from the twigs in autumn. The fall leaf color is wan yellow.

Green Lake's allee of 29 east of the Evans Pool building, planted in the early 1930s, is the most prominent group at the park, although there are 23 additional specimens elsewhere. The largest trunks are 11 feet around. A very unusual specimen is not far from the southwest restrooms. It is enormous, with a less swollen, grayer trunk. Anthracnose affects it more, and it defoliates later. In these respects it is more like the American sycamore.

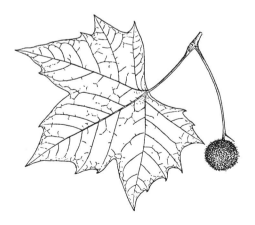

Cherry PLUM
Prunus cerasifera

ACCIDENTS happen, so Green Lake has a Cherry Plum against the south wall of the Bathhouse Theatre. The building's north and west sides are marked by Pissard *purpleleaf* Cherry Plums, but the one intended similarly to decorate the south wall didn't survive—instead, its greenleaf rootstock grew up triumphant, forming a burly-trunked tree.

Cherry Plum, also called Myrobalan Plum, is a native of southeast Europe and Asia Minor. It bears small leaves on greenish twigs, and ripens green, yellow, orange, red or purple plums that are juicy, more or less an inch wide, and a treat to eat in July. It flowers in early March, making a lovely show of pure white blossoms, small individually yet borne in the highest possible profusion. Because the species is hardy, easily raised by seed or cuttings, and accepts grafting so well, it is the preferred rootstock for propagation of both flowering and fruiting plum varieties. It manages sometimes to overwhelm its grafts, so is not at all uncommon. It comes up wild in Seattle. Purpleleaf varieties by the dozens, including hybrids, exist, but only three of them are at Green Lake, as noted on the next two pages.

Moser Purpleleaf PLUM
Prunus × *blireiana* 'Moseri'

FOUR closely planted purpleleaf plum trees grow at Green Lake's east side, near Ravenna Boulevard. They open pale pink, heavy clusters of 15-petaled fragrant flowers in March, then assume their reddish leaf color, which holds all summer. Since the flowers are doubled, few fruit are set. Late July or early August is the season for any plums that do ripen.

This variety originated nearly 100 years ago in France, as a hybrid between the original purpleleaf plum (Pissard's, on the next page), and an ornamental variety of Japanese Apricot. Being a plum-apricot hybrid, 'Moseri' has leaves that are comparatively broad, and its fruit skin is minutely *hairy*. This variety is no longer in nurseries, because a florid pink cousin known as blireiana plum is deemed better. Nonetheless, some people prefer Moser's since it isn't so vulgarly dwarf, muddy colored, twiggily congested, and warty. Moser Plum was named after the renowned Moser nursery family at Versailles.

Pissard Purpleleaf PLUM

Prunus cerasifera 'Pissardii'

FIFTY purpleleaf plum varieties are described in my book on the subject. Pissard's (or *atropurpurea* as some call it) was the original, the one to credit or blame according to your view of these singular creations. In the 1870s, His Majesty the Shah of Persia, employed the Frenchman M. Pissard as a gardener. Pissard knew a good thing when he saw it, or thought he did, and sent to French nursery friends in 1880 the previously unknown *purpleleaf* plum, which was accordingly named after him. The tree differed from regular cherry plum in being larger, with bigger leaves and fruit, besides having colorful leaves. Its ensuing popularity was phenomenal, and the world has since then been the brighter with spring blossoms, and more shadowy during summer, because of the progeny of Pissard's Plum. When it comes to these flowering or ornamental plums, Seattle is one of the most heavily planted areas.

Green Lake has three against the Bathhouse Theatre.

Purple Pony™ Purpleleaf PLUM

Prunus cerasifera 'Purple Pony'™

FACING the road by the caretaker's building by 77th Street at the lake's north end, is a little purpleleaf plum tree. In some respects it is like Pissard's plum (just treated), but its flowers are *pure pink*, not white. The tree is also a dwarf that flowers sparingly, and the unfolding red leaves compete with the scant flowers for attention to a marked degree.

Purple Pony™ Plum originated in California during the late 1950s as a seedling of 'Krauter's Vesuvius' plum. It is not only dwarf and sparing in blossom, but fruitless as well.

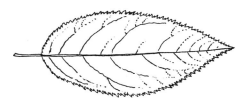

Lombardy Black POPLAR
Populus nigra 'Italica'

STRAIGHT as an arrow and quite as narrow in proportion, Lombardy Poplar is the slender upright sentinel tree that stands out a mile away. Its arresting shape and amazing hardihood have caused it to be planted as much as any tree, on a global scale. Wherever the climate permits, you can see its tall columns, their triangular leaves fluttering in the breeze, then illuminating the landscape in a golden autumn farewell.

This familiar tree is a clone that originated in Italy around 1700. All poplars, aspens and cottonwoods are either male or female, and females alone produce cottony seeds. Fortunately, Lombardy Poplar is male. It is propagated by cuttings and root suckers. Western Washington may have the largest specimens in North America; for whatever reason the tree does exceptionally well here.

Green Lake has five: four larger, and one smaller, all north of the Bathhouse Theatre.

Weeping POPLAR
Populus Simonii 'Pendula'

SEATTLE is the only city I am aware of that is graced by many weeping poplars. The poplar named after M. Eugène Simon, who introduced it from China to France in 1861, is almost never grown in this country except in its narrow upright form or its weeping version, both of which are male clones propagated by cuttings. In China, other named varieties exist, and one is known as Vegetable Poplar (Tsai-Yang) because its young leaves are eaten.

Weeping Simon Poplar has surpassed 100 feet in height in Seattle, although most are nearer half that. The tree is not rare nationally for lack of merit, for it is luxuriously beautiful, flushing light green leaves early in spring, borne on long slender branchlets easily swayed by the wind. Besides its broader leaves, light gray bark differentiates it from weeping willows with their brownish trunks.

Green Lake has thirty, from the boat rental building on the east side, northward and around to the point opposite Duck Island (east of Oak Hill at the northwest part of the park). They are often seen planted in groups of three.

White POPLAR
Populus alba 'Nivea'

DON'T be surprised if you go to see Green Lake's lone White Poplar, southwest of the fieldhouse, and find it *gone*. It is old for a poplar, and may either break in a storm or be cut down before long. Its root suckers, anyway, will persist.

From Europe, north Africa and west Asia, the White Poplar is a variable species, but in our area only two clones are cultivated, this being one. This clone, 'Nivea', is female, releasing cottony seeds May through June. Maplelike leaves, coated on their undersides by a *dense mat of snow-white hairs*, make it completely unmistakable. Bark on young limbs is also creamy whitish, but the Green Lake tree has little of it; its old bark is blackish, deep, and rough.

White Poplar is valued for being one of the hardiest, fastest-growing, most undemanding, pest-free trees of all. On the other hand, it suckers annoyingly and doesn't live very long. As James S. Brisbin, a Civil War general who loved trees passionately, said in 1888:

> This tree is one of the most common throughout our country, and has been planted as an ornamental tree from time to time, but in a little while, instead of being a thing of beauty and a joy forever, it becomes a nuisance, from the number of suckers it throws out.

Coast REDWOOD
Sequoia sempervirens

CALIFORNIA'S coastal redwoods are the world's noblest trees. To grow two hundred feet tall is nothing for them—some are closer to *four hundred*. Their vast, tranquil empire of straight towering red pillars, follows the fog belt for hundreds of miles. We in Seattle are fortunate that this and the other redwoods grow about as well here as in their native haunts. Green Lake has all three species.

Six Coast Redwoods form a grove in the Pitch n' Putt golf course. Their height is not yet special, but the largest trunk, soft in its loose red bark of wonderful thickness, is 13¼ feet around (this book's back cover photograph), and standing next to it, you can *pretend* it soars hundreds of feet into the sky. If you do visit it, by all means also admire the giant European larch nearby.

Dawn REDWOOD
Metasequoia glyptostroboides

DECIDUOUS Redwood or Chinese Redwood are alternate descriptive names for this celebrated tree. After being thought long extinct, it startled science and thrilled the world when it was discovered growing wild in the remote depths of China. In 1948 it was introduced to cultivation in the West, with great fanfare and fuss. Ever since then, Dawn Redwood has amazed everyone with its exceedingly rapid growth. But after all, it *is* cousin to the world's largest trees.

Dawn Redwood has two fascinating characteristics besides its deciduous habit and dramatic tale. First, its swollen, buttressed trunk has odd "armpits" under the branches; these are very deep and practically unique. Secondly, its foliage tastes like carrots—or at least, carrot *greens!* From Bald cypress, also a deciduous conifer in the redwood family, Dawn Redwood differs in putting on its leaves earlier in spring and shedding them sooner in autumn. Also, bald cypress has finer foliage, borne alternately instead of oppositely on the twigs.

Green Lake has three Dawn Redwoods east of the Aqua Theatre, right next to the lake. One is multitrunked. The largest is actually more in the water than on the land, which seems happily appropriate considering that one of the Chinese names for the tree is "Water Fir."

Sierra REDWOOD
Sequoiadendron giganteum

THESE are the Green Lake redwoods that people *notice*, because they number 22, and some are very big—twenty feet around the largest trunk (in the wading pool vicinity).

This is the world's largest tree, fittingly called Bigtree, or Giant Sequoia. Words fail to convey an adequate picture of the tree's mountainous physiognomy. As though emancipated from the usual natural laws governing growth, its rapid spiring ascension is matched by a trunk expansion so extreme that you should really be an eyewitness to comprehend it. Yes, some poplars and eucalypts initially grow as fast—but *they* don't live for thousands of years.

Sierra Redwood is from interior mountainous California, and differs from coast redwood in being bulkier, with especially huge trunks. Its cones are also larger, about walnut-sized. The tree owes its fame to size, but even were it small, it has a ravishingly faultless form, with a mathematically exact taper from stout red base to extreme tip. The healthy green color of its foliage is also handsome. People love planting the tree, and delight in its speed of increase.

During the early 1850s, after the heyday of the California gold rush, the civilized world learned about these mammoth trees, as showmen cut down the biggest trees they could locate, to ship back East and to Europe. Public response was at once fascination and outrage. Henry Thoreau, hearing of this, released his fury in words more passionate than polished (Journal, October 12, 1857):

> This is what those scamps did in California. The trees were so grand and venerable that they could not afford to let them grow a hair's breadth bigger, or live a moment longer to reproach themselves. They were so big that they resolved they should never be bigger. They were so venerable that they cut them right down. It was not for the sake of the wood; it was only because they were so very grand and venerable.

The great writer and counselor of common sense would be pleased to know that John Muir and thousands of other concerned Americans saved the redwoods from lumber mills.

142

SERVICEBERRY
Amelanchier arborea

GREEN LAKE'S first Serviceberry tree was planted in 1991, on the northeast shore, near a bench dedicated to Maury Hagen, Junior. Also in this area, which is not far from Meridian Avenue, is the park's only fig tree. Serviceberry is often called Shadbush, because where it is native back East, it frequently grows along streamsides and opens its tender white blossoms at the same time the shad run upstream to spawn, *i.e.*, in early spring, as larger woodland trees are barely shaking off winter's icy fetters. Only recently have Serviceberry trees been widely available from nurseries. A good thing it is, too, for they are just what people usually need: small, colorful trees that produce berries for birds or humans to enjoy.

During late March, Serviceberry unfolds its silky leaves and nodding clusters of five-petaled blossoms. Notably *narrow* petals make the flowers unlike those of its relatives in the rose family. The leaves lose their hairs and the berries ripen in June or July (Juneberry is a third name of the tree). Fall color is orange or red of lip-smacking beauty. Note: Seattle has a native species of serviceberry, *Amelanchier alnifolia*, that neither closely resembles the Eastern species, nor grows at Green Lake.

SILK TREE
Albizia Julibrissin

EXASPERATINGLY susceptible to coralspot canker, this fine flowering tree is pitiably poor at Green Lake, where nine of them maintain a feeble grip on life. Six face Aurora, between 67th and 70th Streetrs; three are on the southeast shore.

Mimosa and Pink Acacia are other names given to this Old World denizen. The scientific name refers to Filippo Albizzi, a Florentine nobleman who introduced the species to Tuscany in 1749. In 1785 it was brought to the United States. The species, despite its name, is not the one on which silkworms spin their rapturous threads. The name Silk Tree refers instead to its delicate flowers.

Feathery, dainty foliage borne on a broad, light crown, topped by fragrant rosy flower puffs in July and onward, render Silk Tree immensely distinctive and charming. To see it in full bloom is to revel in its splendid, tropical sensuality. We do not have a half-decent lacy and filigreed substitute for it; as far as looks are concerned it's unparalleled. Fortunately, many fair examples can be seen in Seattle. But it does not live long, and is much better off in Portland, where more warmth gives it a keen boost.

Japanese SNOWBELL TREE
Styrax japonicus

SPOTLESS white bell-like blossoms in June make this small tree a cloud of lovely fragrance. During summer it keeps a fresh green appearance, with its reaching sprays of dark shiny leaves, then it yellows and defoliates in autumn. Grayish, felty, hard seedballs drop, too: these pea-sized affairs are ornamentally negligible, poisonous, and give rise to enough offspring as to be weedy. In winter the tree's twiggy crown is fine-textured, but not colorful enough to achieve first-class ranking.

Overall, Japanese Snowbell is a charming flowering tree, that has adequate bearing the rest of the year. Its small size increases its value for home landscapes. So if you love restraint and the subtle touch of *quiet* elegance in your plant compositions, it is indispensable. If instead you derive greater enjoyment from bright fruits or showy fall leaf color, plant something that raises your blood pressure.

Green Lake's only Japanese Snowbell is a 1991 specimen ringed by five evergreen magnolias in the east parking lot's traffic island.

Sorrel TREE
Oxydendrum arboreum

SORREL TREE's leaves in October are like red embers of fire. Redness so clear, so bright, so lustrously reflective, is rare, and ever so welcome at the time of year we're losing our summer sun, and sinking helplessly into the wet, gray days of winter. Similar leaf color is seen in tupelo trees, but not with such gorgeous flowers. For Sorrel Tree or Sourwood has slender, elongated clusters of white lily-of-the-valley flowers in late July, which stay colorful and showy for months as they imperceptibly turn into seeds, accenting the flaming fall leaf-color with creamy yellow splashes. Photographers can't sit still when they see these trees; they *must* get out their gear and click away.

The tree is native in the eastern U.S., and is a member of the same illustrious plant family as rhododendrons, azaleas, and the madrona. It generally is slender and mid-sized, rarely less than 30 feet tall at maturity, or over 50 feet. The bark is pale, furrowed, and a good match for the clean, sharp leaves. In spring, one can nibble the unfolding leaves, which afford a sour taste that some of us relish.

Green Lake has five, all not long in the ground, but they were big when moved. Two are with two hinoki cypresses and a much bigger plume sawara cypress between the Aqua Theatre and parking lot. Two more are northward in the southwest strip, about where West Green Lake Way meets the road to the Aurora underpass. A fifth is in the northeast area of the park, not far from Meridian Avenue.

Colorado SPRUCE
Picea pungens

ERECT, rigid, frightfully sharp needles, short and stout, make this spruce a pain to handle—but their *color* can make the tree an object of such general desire that "blue spruces" by the millions have been planted. Nurseries have cleverly categorized Colorado Spruce seedlings: least desirable, and cheapest, are olive green. Bluish but not especially so are intermediate in esteem and price. Best are "shiners," sporting such vivid baby-blueness that people gladly pay high prices (if they can afford to) for the privilege of owning such a silvery-blue pet.

As its name implies, this spruce is from the Rocky Mountains, so it has the cold hardiness that allows it to be planted in most states. Specimens planted west of the Cascades are smaller and less healthy than their counterparts in Spokane, Wenatchee, etc. Aphids cause it to lose many needles prematurely hereabouts, so people seek powder-blue replacements of other species, which have the added advantage of not having such devilishly prickly needles—white fir, for example.

Fifteen are at Green Lake. Most are fairly blue, but some are green as can be. They differ from the far commoner Norway spruce in being smaller, having short branches, bluish, much stouter needles, and smaller, paler cones.

Norway SPRUCE
Picea Abies

BEFORE the present century, Norway Spruces, as well as some pines and other evergreens, were called *firs*. People would say "spruce fir" much as many of us these days use "pine" very loosely, as when calling practically anything picked up under a conifer a *pine* cone. The ceaseless influence of order-conscious writers and academics has prevailed, to limit the name "spruce" to trees of the genus *Picea*. In this sense, spruces are a comparatively homogeneous group, bearing sharp, short evergreen needles, on rough, scratchy twigs, with lightweight, thin-scaled cones that droop from the uppermost branches, then fall to slowly decay on the ground. Norway Spruce has the largest cones, 5 to 9 inches long, shaped like cucumbers. Its needles are pure deep green and less than an inch in length.

Aside from the silver fir (*Abies alba*, not present at Green Lake), Norway Spruce is Europe's tallest native tree. Its value as a forestry species, and producer of wood, is incalculable. Ornamentally it has been planted widely, for its sweeping long limbs draped in green, and its stately upright habit. The older they get, the more they become unkempt, sparse, and full of horrible dead twigs. It thrives in Seattle.

Green Lake has 73 Norway Spruces, 28 of which are in the Pitch n' Putt golf course.

Oriental SPRUCE
Picea orientalis

EXACTLY the same shape and color as Norway spruce, this differs in having petite needles and smaller cones. You would think it a mere variety rather than a separate species. Ornamentally, it is smaller and neater. The needles are about as short as thumbtacks, but by no means viciously sharp: in fact, they are pleasingly blunt.

Green Lake has only nine. Six are north of the Bathhouse Theatre, right along the main path. A seventh is still farther to the northwest, opposite 76th Street, keeping company with two larches, a yoshino and a horinji cherry. The eighth and ninth are on the lake's southeast strip, north of 65th Street—the latter largest of all.

Sitka SPRUCE
Picea sitchensis

RAINFOREST visitors stand in awe before this mossy Olympian giant, earth's largest spruce by a great margin. Rarely is one tree of a genus so much bigger than any of the others. Sitka Spruce belongs to an elite group of trees which can grow to more than 300 feet tall. The largest trunks require more than 50 feet of tape-measure to encircle. The wood is excellent.This Northwest native is grand in size and much valued commercially. But ornamentally it is inferior to the three species on the previous pages, and to other spruces as well. This is partly because it grows too big: not only does it shoot skyward, its branches cover an unusually wide area. While the needles are lovely, flattened and shiny green on top, contrastingly vivid bluish-white underneath, the twigs they sit on are too commonly ugly with galls, and bare of older needles from the work of aphids.

Sitka Spruce is native in Seattle, but finds moister sites preferable. Many have been planted here, anyway. The fashionable but simplistic sentiment that planting *natives* is necessarily better, can thus result in unappetizing landscapes.

Green Lake has nine in a grove by the northwest parking lot. The largest promises to be of impressive size eventually.

SWEETGUM
Liquidambar Styraciflua

CRUMPLE a leaf from this tree under your nostrils and you will never forget why it's called *sweet* gum. The starfish-shaped leaves release a pleasant resinous odor. Some people viewing the leaf's palmate form, think the tree must be a maple. But maples lack leaf fragrance, and bear their leaves in opposite pairs, not to mention having winged seeds instead of prickly seedballs. Sweetgum trees are in the witch-hazel family. This species is a southern U.S. and Central American native, and becomes a forest tree of great size. Because it is a pestfree, attractive large shade tree, many are planted in cities.

No tree varies more in terms of leaf-color in fall, because it can be *green* until January, or can be pure yellow, orange, red, burgundy—or a riotous mixture—in October. Again, no maple is so uneven. Green Lake's tend to color reddish in late October. Since Sweetgum flowers are inconspicuous, and the seedballs a mere bother, the tree must be appreciated for its foliage.

Green Lake has nineteen, all young. There is a row of thirteen along the southwest strip, one in the northwest area not far from the giant Norway maple, and five with Austrian black pines by the Aqua Theatre.

TULIP TREE
Liriodendron Tulipifera

EVERYONE knows the rainbow-bright, bulbous flowers called tulips. Tulip Trees, however, are a different thing altogether. There are magnolias prized for colorful, large white, rosy or purple April flowers; and there is the tallest deciduous tree of eastern North America. Green Lake has only the huge tree.

Back East this Tulip Tree is frequently known as Yellow Poplar. Botanists dislike the comparison of it to a poplar, but in truth, there are practical similarities that account for such name usage. Besides growing big fast, coloring yellow in fall, and having foliage that ripples wave-like in the wind, the tree has pale, lightweight wood. On the other hand, an extremely odd thing about it is its *leaf shape*. Moreover, it is a bisexual that makes winged seeds, whereas proper poplars are one sex or another, and the females make tiny seeds on cottony threads. Tulip Tree's flowers, also, are not in catkins: look close during June and you may see the rather big greenish flowers, touched with a deft sprinkling of orange.

Green Lake has twenty. Thirteen are street-trees lining the east parking lot's drive. Two are in the vicinity of the wading pool. One is near the southwest parking lot. Far and away the biggest are three in the Pitch n' Putt golf course. You *must* see them. Their size is startling. Note that one consists of a *double* trunk: the smaller, leaning part is highly hazardous and looks as though it may fall down any moment. Nearby is an unblemished single trunk 12 feet around. Stare at their height, and recall that they've achieved such awe-inspiring size in about fifty years' growth! Unlike the other Green Lake Tulip Trees, these golf course denizens have uncompacted soil, which is apparently richer, even though it was once fill dirt.

Black WALNUT
Juglans nigra

Military enthusiasts, perk up: here is a rare treat for you. During the first World War, Black Walnut was the most valuable tree, its precious dark heartwood being used for gunstocks and æroplane propellers. Was it coincidence, then, that this species was chosen for the wholesale planting of street-trees in 1919 to line West Green Lake Way, in commemoration of Seattleites who sacrificed their lives in the war? The Park Commissioner and Board voted to use the trees, even though they could have selected alternate species that would've cost less and performed as well. So, probably the connection was intentional.

Green Lake has fifty-six Black Walnuts, all at the south-southwest area, mostly as street-trees from the Pitch n' Putt golf course to where Aurora thrusts itself against the side of the park. Wild youngsters keep popping up. The October-November nuts are eminently edible, flavorful, nutritious—but to get at them you need to remove a green husk whose dark juicy stains persist for days in human skin, and then must crack a nutshell of rocklike hardness. This may sound dreadful, but if you've never tasted them, they really *are* worth getting to know.

As a wood-producer the species is famous. Its nuts are delicious, too. Yet as a landscape subject it is not so valuable. To begin with, it is difficult to transplant successfully when young because of its plunging taproot. Once established, it grows well and looks as fine as any large shade tree, but its nuts are a nuisance except to those of us who love their flavor. Worst of all, the tree stunts adjacent vegetation. A unique odor pervades its leaves and husks. The Green Lake trees, no doubt because of the poor, compacted earth, are not noteworthy for size. Some others in town are gigantic.

Corkscrew WILLOW
Salix Matsudana 'Tortuosa'

TWISTED branches, twigs and leaves on a broad, upright tree make this curly willow unmistakable even in winter. Other names are Dragon's-Claw Willow and Rattlesnake Willow. Except for its interesting undulating form, it offers little more than a fine-foliaged mass of greenery. Like most willows, it grows rapidly but wears out before long. Many are ugly with disease. Its leaves flush early, stay green late, and finally turn a dull yellow before dropping. The tree is a Chinese clone that doubtless arose as a mutation. It is propagated by cuttings, and has become the most commonly planted willow other than weeping willows and pussy willows. But its disease susceptibility, brittleness, and short lifespan have decreased its friends, so fewer are being planted. 'Golden Curls' and 'Scarlet Curls' are two hybrids which may come to replace it.

Green Lake has two Corkscrew Willows. One is between the lake and the path at about the spot that the lake is *farthest west*, near 65th Street. It is about one-third dead. To its south a ways, is a second, smaller one, near three unsightly giant bushlike Pacific black willows.

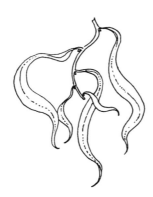

Goldtwig WILLOW
Salix alba var. *vitellina*

GOLDTWIG Willow is among the earth's largest and strongest willows. From Europe, it's been grown a long time in this country, and is more-or-less naturalized here. Both male and female specimens exist, though most in Seattle are male.

Based on observations of the Green Lake trees (over 50), the sexes differ as follows:

Male
-less common at Green Lake
-catkins 2–3 inches
-leaves broader
-leaves hairier
-leaves with finer teeth
-twigs hairy

Female
-more common at Green Lake
-catkins 2–5 inches
-leaves narrower
-leaves less hairy
-leaves with coarser teeth
-twigs only slightly hairy while young

Late April and early May is a good time to view the catkins, should you want to compare them. The beauty of the yellowish-golden twigs is best in late winter.

Pacific Black WILLOW
Salix lasiandra

NATIVE at Green Lake, this tree is very useful to wildlife—many more insects and blights feed on it than on the exotic willows. People can usually recognize it by its ugliness. I counted 23, but am sure to have missed some in the huge thicket of mixed willows at the southern terminus of the lake. Males seem to predominate.

Like goldtwig willow, it is either a giant shrub or a real tree, with no weeping tendency. But its twigs are plain olive green or a bit yellowish, and less stout. Young specimens of the Pacific Black Willow are well-favored with large, dark, glossy leaves, but overall the tree is not handsome enough to be grown for looks; it is not grown in cultivation at all, except where it comes up wild.

Ringleaf Weeping WILLOW
Salix babylonica 'Crispa'

IF every tree were as distinctive as this one, and as literally named, tree-identification would be far easier. Imagine an elegant willow leaf curled in a ring to slip around your finger, and there you have it. Other names reinforce the concept: *Hoopleaf*, *Screwleaf*, and the witty *Ram's Horn Willow*.

Five grow at Green Lake's north end, from north of the Bathhouse Theatre to beyond the caretaker's building by 77th Street. The largest, (shown on this book's front cover) measured in 1988, was 44 feet tall, 48 feet wide, its trunk 6½ feet around. The Ringleaf Willow is a female clone, grown by cuttings. It is not found in nurseries, but should be. The leaves emerge early in spring, and are lightly coated with hairs that persist until the leaves are shed late in fall.

Scouler Pussy WILLOW
Salix Scouleriana

SEATTLE'S most common native pussy willow is conspicuously absent from Green Lake. *One* young female sapling coming up wild, where it is definitely doomed to be cut down, is all I found. It was, in January, 1992, ten feet tall, in a bed behind the Aqua Theatre that officially is planted with three sweetgums, four Austrian black pines, and groundcover of variegated Chinese juniper. (A tough, but impractically crowded plant combination.)

Scouler Willow can grow 80 feet tall. That alone makes it stand out from most pussy willows. Additionally, it can grow on drier sites than Seattle's other two native pussy willows. As an ornamental it is a flop, being plain even when healthy, but usually disfigured by bugs, blights, or fungi.

Sepulchral Weeping WILLOW
Salix × sepulcralis

WEEPING willows are a varied lot. This is among the least pendulous, and is not very common. Green Lake has nine, ranging in size from young wild whips to a marvelous old champion. It's about the first and certainly the last tree, when it comes to leafing out in spring and losing leaves in fall. In December, if not January, it is still partly green. Compared to the weeping willows sold at nurseries, it is not "dripping" enough to capture people's fancy. Vigor and stature it possesses, however, partly from its being a female hybrid between the original weeping willow (*Salix babylonica*) and the white willow. As a graceful lakeside shade tree it is quite superb, even if it doesn't cascade its slender twigs in unison to the water's surface.

Green Lake's giant specimen is about 75 feet tall, and 66 feet wide, with a trunk more than 11 feet around, standing near five larches and some maples on the southeast strip between 63rd and 65th Streets. Two flank the dock by the boat rental building on the east side.

Sitka Pussy WILLOW
Salix sitchensis

LIKE Scouler pussy willow (and the inexplicably missing Piper pussy willow) this is a Seattle native. It is Green Lake's only common pussy willow. At least seven large ones are present, and smaller ones exist. Generally it is a many-stemmed large bush. An old, decrepit little tree hangs on near the water on the southeast shore opposite 65th Street.

The Sitka is differentiated from other pussy willows by its *slender, veiny, dark* leaves which are vividly, luxuriously satin-hairy beneath, borne on conspicuously dark and felty twigs. Also, its catkins are markedly narrow, as well as later to appear than those of the other pussy willow species.

White WILLOW
Salix alba

EXCEPT in its native Europe, the White Willow is usually encountered in cultivated varieties only. Thus the golden willow, the cricketbat willow, and silver willow, are all forms of it that outnumber the original, ordinary form. Well, the plain old White Willow version, in its "unimproved" state, is so rare locally that until finding *one* at Green Lake, I'd seen none anywhere. So the discovery was fun. Compared to goldtwig willow, it has less strength and size, green, hairy twigs, and shorter, darker, quite hairy leaves.

The lone Green Lake individual is jammed together with countless other goldtwig and Pacific black willows forming the extensive thicket at the south end of the lake. Good luck locating it! It is towards the eastern end, not far from a white birch. Since it is unique, maybe we should raise some from cuttings, to test the tree's performance in a less crowded setting.

White WILLOW *hybrid*
Salix × *rubens*

CROSS the White Willow with another European species known as the Crack, Brittle, or Snapping Willow (*Salix fragilis*, not at Green Lake), and the result is super-willows boasting big leaves, fast growth and large size. One such hybrid in the Pitch n' Putt golf course measured 71 feet tall, 59 feet wide, with a burly trunk 12'9" around in 1988, when perhaps 40 years old. But in November, 1991, it broke badly. If the Parks Department doesn't cut down what remains, the crippled tree may live on in a hulking, suckering fashion, for a couple more decades. Except for a smaller, equally broken specimen right next to it, it is the only one of its kind at the park, although even if it is removed roots and all, the simple act of sticking one of its twigs into the ground will resurrect its genetic power in a surging new tree for tomorrow. In case it should be removed, note that a smaller goldtwig willow also lives on the golf course, more to the northeast: its trunk is quite full of holes and has conk fungi growing on it, so maybe it, too, is not long for this world.

WITCH-HAZEL
Hamamelis virginiana

ENGLISH speakers of old called various trees by this name: wych elm, hornbeam, linden, and regular hazel were all sometimes called "witch hazel." But firm literary tradition has settled the name Witch-Hazel on this eastern North American *Hamamelis* species, and also, by extrapolation, to its Asiatic cousins.

Like Seattle's native hazel (*Corylus cornuta* var. *californica*, not present at Green Lake), this is either a shrub or small tree. As its leaves yellow and drop during September and October, it opens small, yellow-golden, threadlike flowers. Look closely or you'll miss them. The tree was formerly much used in folk and herbal medicine, and its twigs used for dowsing divination.

Green Lake has seven that might charitably be called trees, plus others that are hopelessly shrubby. All are in the northwest part. Three are in the bed of cherries and goldenchains west of the Bathhouse Theatre. Two are in a grove of larches by the parking lot. A five-trunked one is in the long, narrow, parking lot bed of cherries and golden rain trees. One is near the four larger golden rain trees.

They can be seen with flowers between mid-September and early December—even into early March during mild winters. Ornamentally they are overshadowed by the Chinese and Japanese Witch-Hazels, that differ in bearing showier, often more fragrant flowers, in the dead of winter instead of in autumn. The Asiatic cousins are less likely to be found growing as trees.

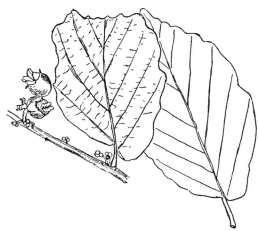

English YEW
Taxus baccata

    TAXOL sounds like a government scheme when you say it, but is really less insidious. Much in the news lately, it is a cancer-fighting drug found in the bark of the Pacific Northwest's native yew tree. English Yew, from Europe, north Africa and western Asia, is deficient in this life-preserving chemical, but *better-looking*. Therefore we may rejoice that Green Lake has the Old World species.

    Yew is a coniferous evergreen with about as dark a green color as exists in the plant kingdom. The trunk is covered in red-brown bark. Many English Yews are bushy, others are 50–90 feet tall with trunks of unbelievable thickness. The females produce juicy red berries enveloping poisonous seeds. Male trees have numerous tiny flowers that make pollen, a yellow, dust-like substance released in late winter and early spring, whose role is to fertilize the female flowers.

    As objects of historic curiosity, and for their wood, yews are priceless. But ornamentally, they can be brooding blackish masses of no finesse or charm. It depends on their location, genetics, size, and degree of human intervention. Usually they are dark blobs; few are attractive trees. Guess which Green Lake's are? You decide. Four are north of the wading pool; three of them are male. One female is on the southeast shore, northwest of where Sunnyside Avenue intersects Green Lake Way, by the gravel perimeter path flanking the road. West of it are two dying native dogwoods.

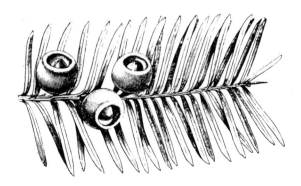

ZELKOVA
Zelkova serrata

How did Zelkova get its name—and the distinction of appearing last in alphabetical tree books? It is simply an honest adaption of the everyday or common name given by the inhabitants of Crete to their native species: as they call it, "Zelkoua." The French botanist Edouard Spach liked it and made it official in 1842. The Cretan species, however, is not in cultivation, at least in this country.

The common U.S. Zelkova is a native of China, Taiwan, Korea, and Japan, introduced to North America in 1862. Its Japanese name is Keyaki. Related to elms, it is similar in having inconspicuously dinky flowers in spring, but even *less* noticeable seeds. It is valued for its branching habit, and for its shapely, toothed leaves. It also makes useful wood. Fall color ranges from an utterly forgettable yellow, to warm, soft orange or rusty red—it is not superb for color, but beats most elms in this feature.

The fifteen Green Lake trees, all by the fieldhouse and bathing beach, show what the chief desideratum of this tree is: its *sublime branching pattern*. To see its silhouette against the sky in winter is to see perfection of line and balance, a dramatic picture of natural artistry.

INDEX

Abies alba 148
Abies cephalonica 86
Abies concolor 88
Abies Nordmanniana 84
Abies Veitchii 87
ACACIA, Pink 144
Acer campestre 107
Acer circinatum 111
Acer macrophyllum 106
Acer palmatum 108
Acer platanoides 'Schwedleri' 109
Acer platanoides 109
Acer Pseudoplatanus 110
Acer Pseudop. 'Atropurpureum' 110
Æsculus × *carnea* 100
Æsculus flava 48
Æsculus Hippocastanum 99
Æsculus octandra 48
Æsculus Pavia 100
Alaska Yellow CEDAR 71
Albizia Julibrissin 144
ALDER, Red 33
Alnus rubra 33
Alpine GOLDENCHAIN 91
Amelanchier arborea 143
American SYCAMORE 133
American White ELM 79
APPLE, European Crab 35
APPLE, Kaido Crab 35
APPLE, Midget Crab 35
APPLE, Orchard 34
APPLE, Purple Crab 36
APPLE, Red Jewell™ Crab 37
APPLE, Redvein Crab 38
APPLE, Siberian Crab 39
APPLE, Turkestan Crab 38
APRICOT, Japanese 135
ARBORVITÆ, Oriental 40
ARBORVITÆ, Pyramidal 41
ASH, Caucasian 42
ASH, Mountain 112
ASH, Narrowleaf 42
ASH, Oregon 14
ASPEN, Quaking 43
Atlas CEDAR 51

Austrian Black PINE 123
Autumn Glory HAWTHORN 93
Bald CYPRESS 67
BEECH, European 44
Betula × *aurata* 45
Betula papyrifera 46
Betula pendula 47
Betula pendula 'Tristis' 47
Betula pubescens 45
Bigleaf MAPLE 106
Bigtree 142
BIRCH, Canoe 46
BIRCH, Downy 45
BIRCH, Downy hybrid 45
BIRCH, Paper 46
BIRCH, Silver 47
BIRCH, Weeping White 47
BIRCH, White 47
Bitter CHERRY 56
Black CHERRY 59
Black COTTONWOOD 66
Black LOCUST 103
Black OAK 113
Black PINE, Austrian 123
Black PINE, Japanese 126
Black POPLAR 137
Black WALNUT 153
Black WILLOW 156
Blireiana PLUM 135
Blue Atlas CEDAR 51
Blue Colorado SPRUCE 147
Blue Lawson CYPRESS 70
BUCKEYE, Ohio 48
BUCKEYE, Red 100
BUCKEYE, Sweet 48
BUCKEYE, Yellow 48
Bull PINE 129
Bur OAK 114
Calocedrus decurrens 53
Canoe BIRCH 46
Carpinus Betulus 98
Castanea species 99
Catalpa bignonioides 50
Catalpa speciosa 49
CATALPA, Northern 49

CATALPA, Southern 50
Caucasian ASH 42
Caucasian FIR 84
CEDAR of Lebanon 54
CEDAR, Alaska Yellow 71
CEDAR, Atlas 51
CEDAR, Blue Atlas 51
CEDAR, Deodar 52
CEDAR, Flat 41
CEDAR, Incense 53
CEDAR, Indian 52
CEDAR, Lebanon 54
CEDAR, Northern White 41
CEDAR, Port Orford 69
CEDAR, Sacred 52
CEDAR, Western Red 55
CEDAR, White 41
CEDAR, Yellow 71
CEDAR, Zebra 56
Cedrus atlantica 51
Cedrus atlantica f. *glauca* 51
Cedrus Deodara 52
Cedrus libani 54
Chamæcyparis Lawsoniana 69
C. Lawsoniana 'Allumii' 70
C. Lawsoniana 'Intertexta' 70
C. Lawsoniana f. *glauca* 70
Chamæcyparis nootkatensis 71
Chamæcyparis obtusa 68
Chamæcyparis pisifera 72
C. pisifera 'Aurea' 73
C. pisifera f. *filifera* 74
C. pisifera f. *plumosa* 74
C. pisifera f. *squarrosa* 73
Cherry PLUM 134
CHERRY, Bitter 56
CHERRY, Black 59
CHERRY, Cornelian 75
CHERRY, Gean 59
CHERRY, Higan 57
CHERRY, Horinji 57
CHERRY, Kwanzan 58
CHERRY, Mazzard 59
CHERRY, Mikuruma-gaeshi 60
CHERRY, Mt. Fuji 62
CHERRY, Naden 60
CHERRY, Ojochin 61
CHERRY, Oshima 61
CHERRY, Pie 63

CHERRY, Shiro-fugen 62
CHERRY, Shirotae 62
CHERRY, Sour 63
CHERRY, Sweet 59
CHERRY, Takasago 60
CHERRY, Temari 64
CHERRY, Ukon 64
CHERRY, Whitcomb 65
CHERRY, Yoshino 65
Cherry PLUM 134
CHESTNUT tree, Horse 99
CHESTNUT tree, Sweet 99
Chinese ELM 81
Chinese PHOTINIA 122
Chinese PINE 124
Chinese REDWOOD 141
Coast REDWOOD 140
Cockspur HAWTHORN 94
Colorado SPRUCE 147
Corkscrew WILLOW 154
Cornelian Cherry DOGWOOD 75
Cornus florida 76
Cornus florida f. *rubra* 76
Cornus Kousa 77
Cornus mas 75
Cornus Nuttallii 78
Corylus cornuta var. *californica* 163
COTTONWOOD, Black 66
Crab-APPLE, Doubleflowered 35
Crab-APPLE, Kaido 35
Crab-APPLE, Midget 35
Crab-APPLE, native 34
Crab-APPLE, Purple 36
Crab-APPLE, Red Jewell™ 37
Crab-APPLE, Redvein 38
Crab-APPLE, Siberian 39
Crab-APPLE, Turkestan 38
Crack WILLOW 162
Cratægus 'Autumn Glory' 93
Cratægus crus-galli 94
Cratægus lævigata 'Paul's Scarlet' 96
Cratægus lævigata 'Punicea' 96
Cratægus monogyna 95
Cricketbat WILLOW 161
× *Cupressocyparis Leylandii* 71
Cupressus macrocarpa 71
CYPRESS, Bald 67
CYPRESS, Hinoki 68
CYPRESS, Lawson 69

CYPRESS, Lawson Blue 70
CYPRESS, Lawson Scarab 70
CYPRESS, Lawson Weeping 70
CYPRESS, Leyland 71
CYPRESS, Monterey 71
CYPRESS, Sawara 72
CYPRESS, Sawara Gold 73
CYPRESS, Sawara Moss 73
CYPRESS, Sawara Plume 74
CYPRESS, Sawara Thread 74
Daimyo OAK 115
Dawn REDWOOD 141
Deciduous REDWOOD 141
Deodar CEDAR 52
DOGWOOD, Cornelian-Cherry 75
DOGWOOD, Eastern 76
DOGWOOD, Eastern Pink 76
DOGWOOD, Kousa 77
DOGWOOD, Pacific 78
Douglas FIR 85
Downy BIRCH 45
Dragon's-Claw WILLOW 154
Eastern DOGWOOD 76
Eastern White PINE 125
ELM, American White 79
ELM, Chinese 81
ELM, Hybrid 80
ELM, Siberian 81
ELM, Smoothleaf 82
ELM, White 79
ELM, Wych 80, 163
English HOLLY 97
English MAPLE 107
English YEW 164
European BEECH 44
European Crab-APPLE 35
European HORNBEAM 98
European LARCH 102
Evergreen MAGNOLIA 104
Fagus sylvatica 44
Ficus Carica 83
FIG, Common 83
FIR, Caucasian 84
FIR, Douglas 85
FIR, Greek 86
FIR, Japanese Alpine 87
FIR, Japanese Silver 87
FIR, Silver 148
FIR, Veitch 87

FIR, White 88
Flat CEDAR 41
Fraxinus latifolia 14
Fraxinus oxycarpa 42
Fraxinus oxycarpa 'Flame' 42
Fraxinus oxycarpa 'Raywood' 42
Gean CHERRY 59
Giant SEQUOIA 142
GINKGO 89
Ginkgo biloba 89
Globe LOCUST 104
GOLDEN RAIN TREE 92
Golden Sawara CYPRESS 73
Goldtwig WILLOW 155
GOLDENCHAIN 90
GOLDENCHAIN, Alpine 91
Greek FIR 86
GUM, Sweet 151
HACKMATACK 102
Hamamelis virginiana 163
HAWTHORN, Autumn Glory 93
HAWTHORN, Cockspur 94
HAWTHORN, Common 95
HAWTHORN, Paul's Scarlet 96
HAWTHORN, Red 96
HAZEL, native 163
HAZEL, Witch- 163
Hedge MAPLE 107
Higan CHERRY 57
Himalayan White PINE hybrid 126
Hinoki CYPRESS 68
HOLLY, English 97
Hoopleaf WILLOW 157
Horinji CHERRY 57
HORNBEAM, European 98
HORSE-CHESTNUT, Common 99
HORSE-CHESTNUT, Red 100
Hybrid Downy BIRCH 45
Hybrid ELM 80
Hybrid PLANE 133
Hybrid White OAK 121
Hybrid White PINE 126
Hybrid White WILLOW 162
Ilex Aquifolium 97
Incense CEDAR 53
Japanese Alpine FIR 87
Japanese APRICOT 135
Japanese Black PINE 126
Japanese LARCH 102

Japanese MAPLE 108
Japanese Red PINE 127
Japanese Silver FIR 87
Japanese SNOWBELL TREE 145
Japanese Tabletop PINE 132
Juglans nigra 153
JUNEBERRY 143
JUNIPER, Rocky Mountain 101
Juniperus scopulorum 101
Kaido Crab-APPLE 35
KEAKI 165
Koelreuteria paniculata 92
Kousa DOGWOOD 77
Kwanzan CHERRY 58
Laburnum alpinum 91
Laburnum anagyroides 90
LARCH, European 102
LARCH, Japanese 102
Larix decidua 102
Larix Kaempferi 102
Lawson CYPRESS 69
Lebanon CEDAR 54
Leyland CYPRESS 71
LINDEN 163
Liquidambar Styraciflua 151
Liriodendron Tulipifera 152
LOCUST, Black 103
LOCUST, Globe 104
Lodgepole PINE 132
Lombardy Black POPLAR 137
London PLANE 133
Magnolia grandiflora 104
Magnolia stellata 105
MAGNOLIA, Evergreen 104
MAGNOLIA, Star 105
MAIDENHAIR TREE 89
Malus baccata 39
Malus domestica 34
Malus fusca 34
Malus × *micromalus* 35
Malus Niedzwetzkyana 38
Malus × *purpurea* 36
Malus Red Jewell™ 37
Malus sylvestris 'Plena' 35
MAPLE, Bigleaf 106
MAPLE, English 107
MAPLE, Hedge 107
MAPLE, Japanese 108
MAPLE, Japanese Purpleleaf 108

MAPLE, Norway 109
MAPLE, Norway Schwedler 109
MAPLE, Sycamore 110
MAPLE, Sycamore Wineleaf 110
MAPLE, Vine 111
Mazzard CHERRY 59
Metasequoia glyptostroboides 141
Midget Crab-APPLE 35
Mikuruma-gaeshi CHERRY 60
MIMOSA 144
Moser Purpleleaf PLUM 135
Moss Sawara CYPRESS 73
MOUNTAIN ASH, Big-berry 112
MOUNTAIN ASH, Common 112
Mountain PINE 128
Mt. Fuji CHERRY 62
Mugo PINE 128
Myrobalan PLUM 134
Naden CHERRY 60
Narrowleaf ASH 42
Northern CATALPA 49
Northern White CEDAR 41
Norway MAPLE 109
Norway PINE 130
Norway SPRUCE 148
OAK, Black 113
OAK, Bur 114
OAK, Daimyo 115
OAK, Dyer's 113
OAK, Oriental White 116
OAK, Pin 117
OAK, Quercitron 113
OAK, Red 118
OAK, Scarlet 119
OAK, Swamp White 120
OAK, White 121
OAK, White hybrid 121
OAK, Yellow 113
Ohio BUCKEYE 48
Ojochin CHERRY 61
Orchard APPLE 34
Oregon ASH 14
Oriental ARBORVITÆ 40
Oriental PLANE 133
Oriental SPRUCE 149
Oriental White OAK 116
Oshima CHERRY 61
Oxydendrum arboreum 146
Pacific DOGWOOD 78

Paper BIRCH 46
Paul's Scarlet HAWTHORN 96
Photinia serrulata 122
PHOTINIA, Chinese 122
Picea Abies 148
Picea orientalis 149
Picea pungens 147
Picea pungens f. *glauca* 147
Picea sitchensis 150
Pie CHERRY 63
Pin OAK 117
PINE, Austrian Black 123
PINE, Bull 129
PINE, Chinese 124
PINE, Eastern White 125
PINE, Himalayan White hybrid 126
PINE, Japanese Black 126
PINE, Japanese Red 127
PINE, Japanese Tabletop 132
PINE, Japanese Umbrella 132
PINE, Lodgepole 132
PINE, Mountain 128
PINE, Mugo 128
PINE, Norway 130
PINE, Ponderosa 129
PINE, Red 130
PINE, Scots 131
PINE, Shore 132
PINE, Tanyosho 132
Pink ACACIA 144
Pinus contorta 132
Pinus densiflora 127
P. densiflora 'Umbraculifera' 132
Pinus Mugo 128
Pinus nigra 123
Pinus ponderosa 129
Pinus resinosa 130
Pinus Strobus 125
Pinus sylvestris 131
Pinus tabulæformis 124
Pinus Thunbergiana 126
Pinus uncinata 128
Pinus Wallichiana hybrid 126
Piper Pussy WILLOW 14, 160
Pissard's Purpleleaf PLUM 136
PLANE, Hybrid 133
PLANE, London 133
PLANE, Oriental 133
Platanus × *hybrida* 133

PLUM, Blireiana 135
PLUM, Cherry 134
PLUM, Moser Purpleleaf 135
PLUM, Myrobalan 134
PLUM, Pissard Purpleleaf 136
PLUM, Purple Pony 136
Plume Sawara CYPRESS 74
Ponderosa PINE 129
POPLAR, Lombardy Black 137
POPLAR, Vegetable 138
POPLAR, Weeping Simon 138
POPLAR, White 139
POPLAR, Yellow 152
Populus alba 'Nivea' 139
Populus nigra 'Italica' 137
Populus Simonii 'Pendula' 138
Populus tremuloides 43
Populus trichocarpa 66
Port Orford CEDAR 69
PRIDE OF INDIA 92
Prunus avium 59
Prunus × *blireiana* 'Moseri' 135
Prunus cerasifera 134
P. cerasifera 'Pissardii' 136
P. cerasifera 'Purple Pony' 136
P. cerasifera var. *atropurpurea* 136
Prunus Cerasus 63
Prunus emarginata 56
Prunus × *Gondouinii* 'Schnee' 63
Prunus 'Horinji' 57
Prunus 'Kwanzan' 58
Prunus Lannesiana 61
Prunus 'Mikuruma-gaeshi' 60
Prunus 'Mt. Fuji' 62
Prunus 'Ojochin' 61
Prunus 'Sekiyama' 58
Prunus serotina 59
Prunus 'Shiro-fugen' 62
Prunus 'Shirotae' 62
Prunus × *Sieboldii* 60
Prunus subhirtella 57
Prunus subhirtella 'Whitcombii' 65
Prunus 'Temari' 64
Prunus 'Ukon' 64
Prunus × *yedoensis* 65
Pseudotsuga Menziesii 85
Purple Crab-APPLE 36
Purpleleaf PLUM, Moser 135
Purpleleaf PLUM, Pissard's 136

Purpleleaf PLUM, Purple Pony 136
Pussy WILLOW, Piper 14, 160
Pussy WILLOW, Scouler 158
Pussy WILLOW, Sitka 160
Pyramidal ARBORVITÆ 41
Quaking ASPEN 43
Quercus alba 121
Quercus aliena 116
Quercus × *Bebbiana* 121
Quercus bicolor 120
Quercus coccinea 119
Quercus dentata 115
Quercus macrocarpa 114
Quercus palustris 117
Quercus rubra 118
Quercus velutina 113
Ram's Horn WILLOW 157
Rattlesnake WILLOW 154
Red ALDER 33
Red HAWTHORN 96
Red HORSE-CHESTNUT 100
Red Jewell™ Crab-APPLE 37
Red OAK 118
Red PINE, American 130
Red PINE, Japanese 127
Redvein Crab-APPLE 38
REDWOOD, Coast 140
REDWOOD, Dawn 141
REDWOOD, Sierra 142
Retinospora 72
Ringleaf WILLOW 157
Robinia Pseudoacacia 103
R. Pseudoacacia 'Umbraculifera' 104
Rocky Mountain JUNIPER 101
ROWAN 112
Salix alba 161
Salix alba var. *vitellina* 155
Salix babylonica 'Crispa' 157
Salix fragilis 162
Salix lasiandra 156
Salix Matsudana 'Tortuosa' 154
Salix Piperi 14, 160
Salix × *rubens* 162
Salix Scouleriana 158
Salix × *sepulcralis* 159
Salix sitchensis 160
Sawara CYPRESS 72
Scarab Lawson CYPRESS 70
Scarlet OAK 119

Schwedler Norway MAPLE 109
Scotch GOLDENCHAIN 91
Scots PINE 131
Scouler Pussy WILLOW 158
Screwleaf WILLOW 157
Sequoia sempervirens 140
SEQUOIA, Giant 142
Sequoiadendron giganteum 142
SERVICEBERRY 143
SHADBUSH 143
Shiro-fugen CHERRY 62
Shirotae CHERRY 62
Shore PINE 132
Siberian Crab-APPLE 39
Siberian ELM 81
Sierra REDWOOD 142
SILK TREE 144
Silver BIRCH 47
Silver FIR, European 148
Silver FIR, Japanese 87
Silver WILLOW 161
Simon Weeping POPLAR 138
Sitka Pussy WILLOW 160
Sitka SPRUCE 150
Smoothleaf ELM 82
SNOWBELL TREE, Japanese 145
Snow CHERRY 63
Sorbus aucuparia 112
SORREL TREE 146
Sour CHERRY 63
SOURWOOD 146
Southern CATALPA 50
SPRUCE, Colorado 147
SPRUCE, Colorado Blue 147
SPRUCE, Norway 148
SPRUCE, Oriental 149
SPRUCE, Sitka 150
Star MAGNOLIA 105
String Sawara CYPRESS 74
Styrax japonicus 145
Swamp White OAK 120
Sweet BUCKEYE 48
Sweet CHERRY 59
Sweet CHESTNUT TREE 99
SWEETGUM 151
SYCAMORE 133
Sycamore MAPLE 110
Takasago CHERRY 60
TAMARACK 102

Tanyosho PINE 132
Taxodium distichum 67
Taxus baccata 164
Temari CHERRY 64
Thread Sawara CYPRESS 74
Thuja occidentalis 'Fastigiata' 41
Thuja orientalis 40
Thuja plicata 55
Thuja plicata 'Zebrina' 56
TULIP TREE 152
Turkestan Crab-APPLE 38
Ukon CHERRY 64
Ulmus americana 79
Ulmus carpinifolia 82
Ulmus glabra 80
Ulmus × *hollandica* 80
Ulmus minor 82
Ulmus pumila 81
Veitch FIR 87
Vine MAPLE 111
WALNUT, Black 153
Weeping Lawson CYPRESS 70
Weeping White BIRCH 47
Weeping WILLOW, Ringleaf 157
Weeping WILLOW, Sepulchral 159
Western Red CEDAR 55
Whitcomb CHERRY 65
White BIRCH 47
White CEDAR, Northern 41
White ELM 79
White FIR 88
White OAK, American 121
White OAK, Oriental 116
White OAK, Swamp 120
White PINE, Eastern 125
White PINE, Himalayan hybrid 126

White POPLAR 139
White WILLOW 161
WILLOW, Black 156
WILLOW, Corkscrew 154
WILLOW, Crack 162
WILLOW, Cricketbat 161
WILLOW, Dragon's-Claw 154
WILLOW, Goldtwig 155
WILLOW, Hoopleaf 157
WILLOW, Hybrid White 162
WILLOW, Pacific Black 156
WILLOW, Piper Pussy 14, 160
WILLOW, Ram's Horn 157
WILLOW, Rattlesnake 154
WILLOW, Ringleaf Weeping 157
WILLOW, Scouler Pussy 158
WILLOW, Screwleaf 157
WILLOW, Sepulchral Weeping 159
WILLOW, Silver 161
WILLOW, Sitka Pussy 160
WILLOW, Weeping Ringleaf 157
WILLOW, Weeping Sepulchral 159
WILLOW, White 161
WILLOW, White hybrid 162
Wineleaf MAPLE 110
WITCH-HAZEL 163
Wych ELM 80, 163
Yellow BUCKEYE 48
Yellow CEDAR 71
Yellow OAK 113
Yellow POPLAR 152
YEW, English 164
Yoshino CHERRY 65
Zebra CEDAR 56
ZELKOVA 165
Zelkova serrata 165

BIRD LIFE of GREEN LAKE

Now that you have *Trees of Green Lake*, all you need to make your library complete is *Bird Life of Green Lake*. This book, to be published in late 1992, will answer your questions about the bird life on and around Green Lake and a variety of related topics. How many species of birds can be found there? What do they eat? Does Green Lake supply this food? What kind of fish are in the lake? Are there reptiles and amphibians? Where do the birds go when they're not here? How many species nest on the lake? Where do they nest? Where do all the male mallards go in summer? How early and how late can we see ducklings on the lake? How do ducks form pairs? When do they form pairs? What type of ducks are all those strange looking ones near the island? Is the island man-made? How old is the lake? Is it a natural lake? Has it always been like it is today? Is the lake polluted or healthy? Why do algae bloom in late summer? How long has that been going on? What is that concrete stand in the southwest corner of the lake?

Biologist Martin Muller has made an extensive study of Green Lake over the past seven years. He leads many bird watching trips around the lake for the Seattle Audubon Society and other groups. This book will include the answers to all the above questions and many, many more. It will deal with bird identification, bird behavior, seasonal changes in the lake's bird population, the lake's geological and human related history and its ecology.

Bird Life of Green Lake is expected to be of the same general size and price as *Trees of Green Lake*. Original line drawings will illustrate many topics.

If you would like to be on the MAILING LIST for more information about the book and an order form (expected late 1992) please print your name and address clearly on a postcard and mail it today to:

Martin J. Muller
6205 Latona Ave. NE
Seattle, WA 98115-6552

You may like to know...

Like most people, the author loves receiving mail. So please write if you are interested in obtaining information. Seize the moment! Schedule tree tours (limit 15 people) for your friends; slide shows featuring bright lovely shots (no murky or glaringly overexposed blights); specific tree consultation or writing services. Additional *Trees of Green Lake* copies and other books can also be ordered. Are you unsure exactly what is being offered, or what cost is involved? Simply ask to receive a free newsletter / information packet. You will be pleasantly surprised.

Green Lake's tree population keeps changing gradually, so eventually this book will need to be revised. You can ask to be notified of any second edition, or can offer information about Green Lake trees for inclusion in such an updated version. Meanwhile, savor the warmth of the sun, refreshment of rain, song of the birds, and fragrance of flowers!

Arthur Lee Jacobson
2215 East Howe Street
Seattle, Washington 98112

Daimyo Oak (see page 115)

WE'RE ONE REASON SEATTLE IS A MOST LIVABLE CITY FOR TREES.

When City Foresters started, hiring a tree service was risky business, especially for your trees. We know. We saw a lot of trees damaged by weather, by disease, and by neglect. We saw a lot more damaged by people, some of them "professionals."

Even if you were lucky enough to find someone willing to post a contractor's bond to protect your house and property, you could still end up with your trees needlessly topped, taken down or otherwise ruined.

And when you consider that a prime tree or trees can add up to 20% of your property's value, aesthetics is not the only issue in responsible tree care.

Things have changed, and we're proud to say City Foresters helped make a lot of those changes. As a charter member of the Northwest Chapter of the International Society of Arboriculture, we were actively involved in drafting standards for tree care for our region, and in developing the certification program currently in place in Washington, Oregon and British Columbia.

And we're happy to see a lot more beautiful, healthy trees in Seattle as a result. That makes a more livable city for all of us.

City Foresters — Seattle's oldest certified, licensed, bonded tree service.

789-5738
CITY FORESTERS, INC.
TREE PRUNING, SURGERY,
REMOVAL & CONSULTATION
CITY F*157P4

- Fine Pruning
- Tree Surgery
- Removal
- ISA Certified Arborists
- Value Appraisals
- Consultation

Member:
International Society of Arboriculture (ISA)
National Arborist Association

14508 Whitman Ave. N.
Seattle, WA 98133
(206) 367-4048

SEATTLE TREE PRESERVATION

ARBOREAL SERVICES INC
Tree Care Professionals

Fine Pruning
Precision Removal & Stump Grinding
Consultation, Appraisals

Members of the International Society of Arboriculture

Our Practices Recognize the National Standards
Set by the NAA & ANSI for Quality & Safety

523-6166
914 NE 65th • Seattle, WA 98115

I.S.A. CERTIFIED
ARBORISTS #28